Comments by Readers of The Healer Is You

"Diane See's *The Healer Is You*, is an excellent guidebook into the emerging landscape of the new medicine. It is becoming clear that we cannot be whole without attention to all we are—body, mind, spirit. This books shows why."

— Larry Dossey, M.D., author, *The Power of Premonitions*

"A valuable contribution to our growing awareness of the interaction between the body and the mind."

— Jean Liedloff, author, *The Continuum Concept*

"This book is clear, simple and personally stated, yet well researched with many good authors and teachers quoted. The part about child abuse is unusual in a how-to-take-care-of your-body book, but I was caught by the wisdom and the kindness in the way it is presented. It could encourage many folks to begin their own healing."

— Lynn Scott, former Director Children's Program, Center for Attitudinal Healing

"I was struck by how personal the tone of the book is. As if the author is talking directly to ME. She speaks simply about profound matters, and gives references to look up if I want to delve further. It is such a gracious reminder of things thought of before, but forgotten in our busy lives."

— Eve Langton, Social Worker, Therapist

"I am reading this wonderful book *The Healer is You*. It is so simple to understand and is helping me so much in my dealings with my life, my world, and more. I am taking time to breathe, to reflect, to imagine, to heal."

— Mary Thomas, teacher

"This book is as good as I have seen, and better than most. Not only does Diane seem to cover everything but her personality is in every sentence."

— Tam Greene

D1713559

THE HEALER IS YOU

Understanding Mind-Body Medicine

Diane See

THE HEALER IS YOU: UNDERSTANDING MIND-BODY MEDICINE

ISBN: 978-0-9856544-0-5

Edited and designed by Ted Cabarga

dianesee@icloud.com

To the memory of
Jean Liedloff

"Patients carry their own doctor inside. They come to us (doctors) not knowing that truth. We are at our best when we give the physician that resides within each patient a chance to go to work."

Albert Schweitzer, M.D.

"Our body is self-correcting, equipped with its own personal pharmacy that manufactures what it needs for healing and controls all its systems. It repairs itself, to a point. It regulates itself, to a point."

Christiane Northrup, M.D.

"Eighty percent of symptoms are self-diagnosed and self-treated without professional care. The first step to improve the healthcare system is to improve patient competency."

David Sobel, M.D.

CONTENTS

CONTENTS (continued)

HEALING PRACTICES

FOREWARD

Many years of research efforts and clinical experiments have led to a new approach in medical science that recognizes that the mind, with its thoughts, emotions and attitudes, has a central impact on the health of the body. What is more, it has been shown that by paying attention to our mental states we can learn to control them. *THE HEALER IS YOU: Understanding Mind-Body Medicine,* brings the subject of self-healing to life with personal examples and quotes from experts in the field of mind-body medicine. This book is an attempt to show how to use these natural and harmless methods in your life.

When we become ill, we usually think only about treating the physical body. But the body is only one part of who we are. That is why I suggest we look more deeply. In the following chapters we will examine each of the four main aspects of our lives to see how they work together for health and happiness.

First, we will focus on the quite obvious influence of the physical aspect, and simple, natural ways to optimize the health of the body. Then we will consider the more abstract influence of the mental aspect, and consider "reprogramming" our minds to help in achieving our goals. Next we will delve into the mostly hidden influence of the emotional aspect, how negative emotions can damage the body and how to free ourselves from their grip. Finally, we will consider a spiritual way of looking at life that may allow us to enjoy a harmonious state where health, happiness and inner peace come naturally.

Knowledge of the mind-body connection, and its use in healing, goes back to the ancient traditions of China and India, and shamanic traditions from Africa, South America and the Native North Americans. These healing systems, typically combining nutrition, herbs, breathing techniques, movement, meditation and a belief in a Divine power, are still being practiced around the world. Along with modern scientific discoveries, these traditional practices are demonstrating that the body and mind are part of an intelligent system involving the brain, the nervous system and the immune system. The scientific term for this is psychoneuroimmunology, or PNI. Although still somewhat controversial, the evidence of this interconnection is changing the face of health care.

This book attempts to cover the basic principles and techniques of "mind-body medicine" in everyday terms. Although simple it is comprehensive, more practical than technical, more experiential than theoretical. With the dizzying number of books and articles about health on the market, this book brings together all the essential concepts and techniques of self-healing, and shows how they can be applied on a daily basis. It is based on the curriculum I designed for a course called "Mind-Body Health" that I taught at City College San Francisco between 1990 and 2003. Hundreds of men and women of all ages practiced these suggestions with great benefit. My desire is to reach more people with this positive and hopeful message.

The recommendations offered here are for everyone. Whether you are young or old, healthy or sick, under medical care or not, you will see that you have the ability to improve your life because ultimately, the healer is you. Only you can decide how you will take care of yourself each day. Follow this natural way to health and happiness in your own time. You may start from the beginning and read it through, or read one section at a time. Or you may prefer to skip around and read what interests you the most. After the cost of this book, the rest is free. You might think of it as a bedside book to read at a quiet time when you can relax and contemplate the concepts proposed.

Diane See   Santa Cruz, California   2012

PRINCIPLES OF SELF-HEALING

Designed for Survival

The first principle is that self-healing is possible because we are designed for survival. We come equipped with everything we need to stay well—a blueprint for growth and development with an intricate system of checks and balances, and a plan for self-correction. This complex instrument includes all the systems that keep us alive—the digestive system, the respiratory system, the circulatory system etc., plus a healing system that takes care of repairing broken skin and bones, fighting off germs, filtering and eliminating toxins, and continually renewing and replacing damaged cells. What's more, the brain is a kind of pharmacy that dispenses the chemicals required to carry on the many functions of the body, in the right proportions and with no side effects. And all of this runs on automatic, outside of our conscious awareness.

Yet, as caretakers of this living vehicle called the body, it is important to understand how it operates, so as to provide the proper preventive maintenance. So perfect is the design, that it even provides built-in reminders so that we don't forget to do our part. For example, the sense of thirst reminds us to provide the body with water, hunger doesn't let us forget to provide fuel, and the pain response provides the "flashing red warning lights" that call for our attention when something goes wrong.

In every area of our lives, actually, problems can be seen as blessings in disguise, because they alert us to what needs to change. In other words, pain and suffering are part of the self-correction system. Any condemnation or judgment or worry about the disturbance only creates more disharmony.

We would never neglect our expensive new car, counting on the repair service to fix it after it breaks down, yet many people neglect their bodies expecting the doctors to fix them after they become sick. Why not take care of this incredible mechanism on a daily basis, instead of thoughtlessly mistreating it and expecting to get patched up later? Good preventive maintenance can build a strong internal healing system which is more able to resist viruses, toxins, or even the effects of bad genes!

I am not suggesting we can live forever, but I am proposing that there is a perfect plan at work, and our job is to help it along. Just as filmmakers "take" a scene over and over until they get it just right, in our lives we have "miss-takes" too. That is nature's way of teaching us, through the logical consequences of our actions, what works and what does not. Knowing that the body we live in comes equipped with a system for correction, we pick ourselves up, brush ourselves off, remember what didn't work, and change course.

This first principle tells us that we are designed to stay healthy, and that our bodies are always working toward our good. The essential part we are meant to play is to cooperate with the built-in system. Knowing this, we can relax and rejoice.

Harmony in Mind and Body

The second principle is that self-healing is possible when we are in a harmonious state. When we take good care of our physical bodies, keep our minds clear and positive and our emotions calm, and when we are spiritually at peace, the body functions as it was meant to—smoothly and efficiently.

Everything we do and say and think and feel counts. It isn't enough to eat healthy food if we harbor anger and resentment toward others. Constant hostility has been shown to disrupt the heart rate and can lead to heart disease. On the other hand, feelings of gratitude and appreciation could prevent heart disease. Taking time to quiet the mind for even a little while every day can lower blood pressure, reduce tension, overcome insomnia and lower cholesterol levels. Taking a few deep breaths can quickly control anxiety, improve concentration and calm us down. Social support can increase longevity. It is all connected.

Unavoidably however, there are external forces acting upon us every day that disrupt the natural harmonious balance. Accidents and injury, excessive noise, extreme climate changes, family conflicts, fears and worries and myriad other disturbances, upset the system's balance, touching off a series of reactions and symptoms that can lead to illness. The body goes about its business of repairing, replacing and adjusting in a million little ways, trying to maintain life as long as it can, while we carry on our daily activities oblivious to what is going on inside. It does this day in and day out, from birth to death. When destructive forces become too much for the body to handle they begin to take a toll on our health. The good news is that we can learn to focus our attention on the positive things in life as much as possible, and return to a state of harmony.

Why is it that we find ourselves so often in a state that is contrary to the natural order? Perhaps it is because our God-given free will honors us with the respect and the opportunity to make bad choices as well as good ones, so we can learn the difference. It is always up to us. It can't be forced. Force has never been a good way to learn. Free will balks at coercion. Can you force yourself to be peaceful? Or relaxed?

This principle shows that we are most healthy when the mind and body are interacting harmoniously. By returning to that state of natural balance as often as possible, we can eliminate the obstacles to peacefulness and good health.

A Way of Life

This principle is that self-healing is possible when we actually live and practice a healthy approach to life. Have you heard about the man who goes to the doctor and says, "Doctor, I don't feel well," and the doctor says, "Have you tried giving up everything you enjoy?" Trying to stay healthy usually has such negative connotations—about all the things we shouldn't do, or things we're supposed to do, things to watch out for and things to avoid. It's no fun. That is why I propose that we think of health not only as the absence of illness or symptoms, or a list of dos and don'ts, but rather as a healthy way of life.

Creating health is more than the usual Western approach, which is to take medicine after becoming sick. As was written in an ancient Chinese medical textbook, "To treat after one is diseased is like waiting until one is thirsty to begin digging a well." Rather, we can practice preventive health, and as prescribed in the same Chinese text, "polish every stone" that builds the temple of our bodies. That is, we try to avoid conditions that lead to the breakdown of the body and give it the best materials we can. We learn to use little problems as reminders to adjust some of our habits so as to restore harmony before little problems become big ones. When challenges come, we can use mind-body methods to help.

If you are serious about practicing self-healing, think about starting a journal, calendar diary, or even just a little notepad for keeping track of any persistent symptoms or feelings, physical as well as emotional. This will be beneficial for your own self-assessment. You can note significant events in your life, your health routines, medications (if any) and remedies taken. Become aware of your current lifestyle habits and note it all in your new health and healing journal—what you eat, how much you sit around or move around, and what kinds of thoughts occupy your mind throughout the day. That will help you begin to see what makes you feel good and what does not help. When you get a medical check-up, your personal notes can be valuable information for your doctor.

And don't forget to keep track of the things you are grateful for every day. Many people keep a gratitude journal to help them focus on what is positive in their lives.

Design your own plan or schedule, or just stick a reminder note on your refrigerator saying "Breathe." If you realize one day that you had forgotten all about self-healing for a week or two, or had broken your resolve to exercise every day, just reconsider your goals and begin again when, or if, you are ready. No guilt, no hurry. Think of it as a lifelong journey, a continual practice rather than a goal to strive for. Striving can be good motivation, but be sure it doesn't lead to feelings of failure or guilt or defeat.

As you can see, the third basic principle is about doing it! If any of these suggestions feel right to you, begin to slowly incorporate them into your daily life. If you want the benefits, it is up to you to act on them. This is not a new health regime requiring time and discipline. If you see the truth in it, it can be an adventure—a new way of living.

8   The Healer is You

Part One

Body

Dancing through Life

"Attention changes the state of muscles—not movement."
Moshe Feldenkrais

Starting with the understanding that the body is only one part of who we are—the vehicle or instrument through which we live—this section will focus on clearing and tuning up the instrument for better functioning. When cleared of obstructions and properly maintained, our true essence, or inner self, can come through and express itself with freedom and joy. This physical body is here to serve us, but often we take it for granted and neglect its needs. Here we will discuss the importance of proper alignment and release of muscle tension for increased ease of movement, and how the mind can help to achieve those goals. I will begin by relating some personal experiences.

Throughout my teens, studying modern dance was my greatest joy, and an education in movement and proper use of the body. Yet I couldn't get rid of my tight muscles no matter how I tried. Twenty-five years and five children later I returned to serious dance training, and in the process I learned the importance of the mind-body connection. To my surprise, I discovered that my physical limitations were not as fixed as I had previously thought. Despite my age, I became looser and stronger.

One day one of my dance teachers encouraged me to demonstrate an exaggerated expression of joy, as if on stage. With head thrown back, chest lifted, arms in the air, the muscles in my back spontaneously let go. Suddenly, my spine straightened, my neck lengthened and my shoulders dropped. It was like a miracle I was certain those muscles were locked in forever, but in that moment they were permanently set free—solely by a thought. In a different class, tension in my leg muscles prevented me from achieving a certain dance pose. One night I dreamed that I accomplished the position, and felt the ease of it. The next day in class I relaxed into the pose comfortably and naturally! From that time on it was no problem. These incidents taught me that physical limitations are often mental or emotional.

The next surprise was that as the muscles of my body released their grip and my posture improved, my mind also let go of some of its limitations and fears. My new image expressed a relaxed self-confidence. Studies of the mind-body connection show that your mind believes what your body is telling it, as well as the other way around. An old Peanuts cartoon shows Charlie Brown standing with his head and shoulders drooped forward. He is saying, "If you want to be depressed you have to stand like this." In the next frame he straightened up and said, "If you stand up straight you can't be depressed." Charlie wisely recognized the connection between posture and emotions, and how intentionally changing one affects the other.

Mention of the word "posture" usually causes a guilty reaction, causing people to suddenly straighten up stiffly. Most of us remember being told to "Stand up straight!" We threw our chest out, chin up, shoulders pushed back, neck tense. Military posture might work in the military, but in daily life we want a more natural, comfortable posture so we can move with less effort and less pain and prevent stress-related illnesses. Try the Gentle Alignment practice near the end of this chapter, where you will learn to align the bones and relax the muscles, allowing for greater ease of movement.

T'ai chi is a form of exercise that focuses on releasing tension in the muscles and joints and aligning the bones, to achieve a more comfortable and stable posture. It is a martial art that originated in China, now being practiced all over the world by people of all ages, for calming the mind and the body. The slow flowing movements allow the life force energy, called "chi," to freely circulate through the body and increase inner strength. The health benefits of regular practice of t'ai chi are well documented. I have been teaching and practicing T'ai Chi Chih™ since 1995. This gentle but effective form is based on the principles of traditional t'ai chi, but is designed as a meditation in motion rather than a martial art.

Yoga, like t'ai chi, is a mental and spiritual, as well as a physical practice. Both of these traditional forms offer a total approach to health that affects all the systems in the body—balancing the mind, the body and the emotions, and bringing inner peace and relaxation. There are many styles of yoga, ranging from simple, slow stretches to very energetic and intense practices. Each style is valuable, depending on the individual's physical condition. It is always important to focus on relaxing the muscles and easing into the postures, to avoid injury.

In fact, any kind of physical exercise can be improved with attention. Professional athletes and dancers use focused attention to perform great physical feats. Arnold Schwarzenegger, a weight-lifter before his subsequent careers in acting and politics, said, referring to the practice of pumping blood into muscles by lifting weights, "A pump with your mind in it is worth ten with your mind out of it. If your mind is drifting it's not as effective as when your mind is in it." Rather than distracting the mind while working out, by listening to music or thinking about our problems, we can pay attention to our breathing, and our posture, and the way we are moving.

Many of us are still holding tension in muscles that we contracted at one time for protection from unpleasant life experiences, but then forgot how to release. In his book *Betrayal of the*

Body, Alexander Lowen, M.D. referred to this type of muscle tension as "armoring," using the tightened muscles as a shield. If this condition continues it causes the muscles to become rigid and the joints to stiffen up, which makes moving more of an effort. Armoring also tightens the diaphragm muscle, limiting how deeply we can breathe. Limited breathing then leaves us feeling anxious, and can cause new emotional problems.

Moshe Feldenkrais, the French bodywork pioneer, in his book *Awareness through Movement,* describes his unique system of improving the functioning of muscles, and the whole body, with focused attention on very small movements. He says this approach can change the state of muscles.

Some form of movement is a natural part of a healthy life. In the old days, before cars and modern conveniences, people walked long distances, chopped wood and carried water. Now most of us have to simulate hard work. We call it exercise. Although we all know it is important, exercising is very easy to avoid. On the other hand, we don't want to overdo it and wear ourselves out before our time. Rest is also important.

Choose a form of exercise appropriate for your level of fitness, to strengthen your heart and keep your blood vessels open, as well as naturally improving your breathing. It prevents the loss of muscle tissue that leads to weakness, and it burns excess fat. Contrary to common logic, exercise prevents joints from wearing out and builds bones, so even when there is some joint damage, gentle movement may bring improvement.

If you are too busy for regular exercising, try to find creative ways to fit some sneaky exercises into your life. Instead of feeling impatient while standing in line at the post office, or waiting for a bus, you can do some little knee bends, or slowly raise up on your toes a few times. Stand with your weight equal on both feet instead of slouching, check your alignment and balance and take some deep breaths. When you are walking, and even while driving, practice aligning your head and shoulders and letting go of muscle tension. You will take deeper breaths and feel more alert and awake. While watching television or talking on the phone you can lift and drop your shoulders several times, or lift your legs one at a time, repeatedly.

Exercise shouldn't be a chore. Keep moving in the ways you enjoy the most, whether it is soccer or volleyball, swimming or dancing, yoga or t'ai chi, running, working out at the gym, or simply walking. The more you enjoy it the more likely you will do it, and it will do you the most good. My goals when I exercise, whether it is dancing, practicing T'ai Chi Chih, or walking (my three favorite ways to move), are to be aware of my posture, relax my muscles, loosen my joints and breathe.

Whatever you do, the following practice will prepare you for relaxed and balanced movement. Stop for a moment after each suggestion. Use your imagination as much as possible. I suggest you read the whole exercise through before you begin.

GENTLE ALIGNMENT

Stand with your feet slightly apart (or sit in a straight-backed chair).

Take a few deep breaths, slowly in and out. Then, on an in-breath, imagine filling your whole body with air, as if you are a person-shaped balloon. Feel your entire torso expand, your legs and your arms becoming empty and light. Exhale slowly and completely. Repeat. Continue to breathe normally, retaining the sense of lightness.

Looking straight ahead, gently lift your head toward the ceiling, lengthening the back of your neck and your spine. With your head lifted from the top, your chin is

neither dropped nor pushed forward. It pivots easily on top of the small vertebrae in the neck.

Imagine a cord extending upward from the base of your spine to the top of your head, continuing upward and attaching to the ceiling (or the sky). Or, you may picture a skeleton in a laboratory hanging from a hook, bones dangling limply. Take a few minutes to visualize your muscles melting until you feel like a skeleton (or a marionette, if you prefer). Notice that without muscles there is nothing to be tense. The bones slowly settle into their most natural and balanced positions.

Your shoulders are dropped, neither pulled backward nor slumped forward. Your arms and hands hang loosely at your sides. Your rib cage and pelvis hang suspended from your spine.

Legs, knees and ankles are relaxed, joints are loose. Picture the bones connected to each other only by thin string. Still lifted by the imaginary cord, feet are planted on the ground, giving a feeling of stability. Muscle tension continues to melt down to your feet into the earth.

Remain standing (or sitting) for a few minutes, and notice how you feel. When you are ready, walk around a little bit and see if you feel any different.

This simple exercise can be put into practice at any time. It takes some attention and awareness to keep your body in good balance. Use a full-length mirror as a guide. While going through your daily activities, try to remember to "breathe, lift and melt."

I have found that climbing stairs or hills become almost effortless when I remember to focus on the bones. A balanced posture reduces the work the muscles have to do to maintain the body in an erect position. When it is gently aligned, moving is easier, and exercise is more enjoyable. It is also the most graceful and attractive posture.

Always try to give your body encouragement and reassurance. You can think, if not actually say out loud (in private), "You're doing fine, body. Keep up the good work!" Try not to see your body as the enemy, falling apart, hurting, gaining weight, getting old, or getting sick—even if it is—because it is responding to your thoughts. It is never too late to think healthier and move better. With your support and attention your body will serve you for a long time, and allow you to dance your way through life.

Eating for Body and Soul

"Natural food is food that has been alive fairly recently!"
Andrew Weil, M.D

For some people, food is nothing but fuel, and of course it is the fuel that keeps our bodies running. But for me, it's more. I love to eat it, cook it, talk about it and grow it. I especially love to pick it. If I can pluck a lemon from a tree, eat a strawberry from my garden, or gather nasturtium blossoms to brighten up a salad, I'm happy. But my main interest is natural food—the best fuel.

All foods are natural in the sense that they are derived from the only source there is—nature, but when that food has been processed in unnatural ways, and preserved with chemicals and additives and other artificial ingredients, most of the nutrients have been destroyed, or altered.

Modern agriculture, and imports from countries around the world, have revolutionized our eating habits. While we all enjoy the variety, the accessibility and the abundance of packaged pre-cooked food, a growing movement of health-minded people is encouraging the return to eating food that is grown locally, raised organically, eaten seasonally and unprocessed. In the colorful words of Andrew Weil, M.D., the well-known author of *Why Health Matters*, and other books on mind-body healing, the food we eat should have been "alive fairly recently." In other words, fresh!

When you think of the body as being composed of trillions of cells that make up your bones, muscles, heart, lungs, skin and every single part of you, you must conclude that it is important to take good care of those cells. The foods you eat are the building materials for the body. Our species, like all others, is designed to expect a certain wide range of nutrients that will give the body what it needs for its optimal growth and development. Not just anything will do. If you don't ingest enough of the right kinds of foods, the cells will be deficient and not function properly, leading to illness. If you eat too much of foods that contain artificial or toxic ingredients, it will disrupt the normal processes of the cells and lead to physical breakdown.

As we know, an automobile engine is very carefully designed to make use of a specific kind and quality of fuel and no other. We would never intentionally put any foreign matter into our fuel tanks. Recently a friend of mine accidentally put diesel fuel in her car. It died a few minutes later on the highway and was very expensive to repair. Could our bodies be less carefully designed? Although we obviously have a wider menu to choose from, could the kind and quality of foods we depend upon to make us run, be less important? If not for the fact that we are self-healing, self-correcting beings, some of us surely would be in the junkyard by now.

As it is, the body makes a herculean effort to deal with all the junk food we put into it. It adjusts, it filters out the toxic chemicals as well as it can, and makes do. But that takes its toll, putting tremendous strain on the liver (the body's main filtration plant), damaging the cells and the immune system, and playing havoc with the delicate balance of hormones that control the body's systems. Eventually the body loses the battle, often sooner than necessary. Eating natural foods grown in your own area, and in season, is healthier for you as well as being fresher and less expensive.

Several decades ago, Rachel Carson wrote her classic book, *Silent Spring*, warning of the diseases that would result in the future from the poisonous pesticides sprayed on the food crops, the chemical fertilizers added to the soils, and the preservatives in the processed foods. There is evidence of her predictions now, in the high rate of chronic diseases seen in younger and younger people, and the increased incidence of cancer. Since she wrote that book, food suppliers have developed even new ways to alter the plants and animals we eat in an attempt to increase production and shelf-life—not to mention profits. Among these are genetic modification, irradiation and trans fats. The long-range effects of these processes may be very dangerous. If there is even a chance of that, I try to avoid these foods.

There is no one right way to eat that everyone should follow, so I will not offer specific dietary suggestions. We have different body types, blood types, lifestyles, cultural preferences, genes, age, health conditions, allergies, beliefs, likes and dislikes and many other differences that affect our eating habits. Obviously, the subject of nutrition is filled with controversy as well as mis-information, and many people are confused. There is too much to say about this for the scope of this book, so you may want to do some research to see what attracts your interest. But re-member the words of Mark Twain, "Beware of reading about health—you might die of a misprint."

Experts on aging tell us that for a longer life we are better off when under-satisfied. They say we should eat to the point of feeling energy, instead of feeling lethargic from satiation. Di-gestion works more efficiently when the stomach is not too full. Eating slowly, and chewing well, gives the body a chance to register when we have had enough. If we eat too quickly and don't pay attention, we will ignore the subtle signals and miss the inner warnings.

I had been teaching the importance of "listening to your body" as a guide to knowing what it wants and needs, when after class a student told me excitedly that at a restaurant the night before her body suddenly spoke to her. "Really," I said, "what did it say?" "It said STOP!" she said with delight. "And I did!" I congratulated her on listening to her inner voice.

No matter how healthy our food, without proper digestion we cannot get all its benefits. Digestion begins in the mouth, where food is ground up and mixed with the digestive enzymes in saliva. Thorough chewing, besides helping set the pace for slower and calmer eating, assures that we will absorb the nutrients the food contains. It is a good idea to swallow each bite before taking the next bite. Surprisingly however, while it is necessary to thoroughly chew all plant foods (grains, fruits and vegetables), animal foods are digested by hydrochloric acid in the stomach, rather than in the mouth, and need minimal chewing. Think about carnivorous animals in the wild that don't take time to chew.

Unlike wild animals however, it is best to sit down when you eat. If possible, sit for a few minutes both before and after meals. Probably most harmful to our digestion, and therefore our general health, is to eat when we are upset or rushed. As we will see, the body is designed to temporarily shut down the digestive system during stressful circumstances.

Don't forget to drink as much pure water as you can. Every cell in your body depends on adequate water in order to perform its normal functions. It is especially important for the brain. Water is essential for digestion and the absorption of food, and helps eliminate digestive wastes. It flushes the system and cleanses the cells of toxins. Aim for six to eight cups a day, but do the best you can. Don't be like a forgotten plant, drooping and withering.

While the science of nutrition focuses on nourishing the body, there is a deeper part of us that also needs to be fed. Food should serve both body and soul. The body needs vitamins and other nutrients, but what the soul needs is ambience. How do you eat for the soul? Well here again, it is about awareness. You will get more satisfaction from your meals if you take the time to taste, to savor, to notice your food. Perhaps some soft music would be more conducive to good digestion than watching violence on television while you eat, or reading the newspaper. If you have to eat on the rush sometimes, even a moment of recognition of the food being eaten, and appreciation of it, helps a lot.

Some attention to the table setting, too, can help calm your mind. How about a few flowers on the table—even if it is only some dandelions in a soda bottle. Have you been saving your good china and crystal for some very special guest? You be the guest of honor! Set a luxurious table for yourself or your family once in a while, or invite someone to share a meal with you.

Color also plays a part in feeding the soul as well as the body. A harmonious color scheme on the plate, as well as in the place setting, gives a feeling of peacefulness, which in turn, improves digestion. Nature has endowed fruits and vegetables with deep beautiful colors, and we now know that these colors not only feed the soul but they contain "phyto-chemicals" that protect the body against cancer and other diseases. It seems that each color—green, orange, yellow, red, or blue—counteracts disease from a different angle. We are designed to be attracted to the foods that do us the most good. There is probably no greater boon to health than to eat a variety of different fruits and vegetables every day, both raw and cooked, to get the most of nature's protection.

With all of this in mind, I encourage you to consider the importance of eating natural foods to help you live longer, look better, have greater endurance, resist infection and overcome illness. Appreciate the wonderful fuel nature provides for us. A grateful attitude is good for your health as well as for your soul. Go slowly when making changes, and if you realize your diet falls short of perfection, don't feel guilty. Guilt creates stress.

Remember to indulge your desires once in a while, because constant deprivation leads to rebellion. The soul likes to enjoy. Keep in mind however, that the food you eat contains the nutrients that feed every cell in your body and make it run. You wouldn't want to build your dream house out of cheap materials would you? What about the temple of your spirit?

Breath Is Life

"Whoever breathes most air lives most life."
Elizabeth Barrett Browning

We can survive weeks without food, and days without water, but we can't last more than a few minutes without air. Breath is life. In order for us to live, our lungs need to continually take in oxygen and release carbon dioxide. Fortunately, breathing is an automatic process so we don't have to worry about forgetting to do it. Imagine if you had to think, "Now when was it that I took my last breath?" There is a survival factor in having breathing be involuntary, but also in the ability to control the breath voluntarily, such as when under water. Breathing is the only basic bodily function that gives us this conscious control.

One of my students asked, "Why do I need to learn about breathing when I've been doing it all my life?" Good question. But chances are most of us are not breathing well enough. Babies breathe correctly instinctively—freely from the belly—but most people lose that ability as they grow up and the stresses of life cause us to clench our stomach muscles. Over time that tension can get locked in, making it hard to expand the lungs completely, and we end up taking only short breaths. On the other hand, life can be too easy. We sit around too much and don't exercise enough. It is true that we breathe well enough to stay alive, but probably not well enough for optimal health.

Take a few moments to observe your breathing just as it is, without trying to fix it. Stop reading for a few moments and notice how your breath is moving in and out. As you pay attention to it, see if it deepens naturally. If it seemed that you were hardly breathing at all, you're not alone. Most people find that their breathing is very shallow. The important thing at this point is not to judge what you find, but just to become aware.

The following simplified description of how breathing works may encourage you to practice breathing more effectively: Picture the air coming in through the nostrils and going down through the bronchial tubes into the lungs, where it deposits oxygen. As the bloodstream passes through the lungs, it picks up the oxygen and carries it to the heart where it is pumped throughout the body. The bloodstream is like a freight train bringing oxygen and essential nutrients to every cell in the body. On its way it picks up carbon dioxide, the natural waste product from each cell, and deposits it in the lungs. When we exhale, the toxic waste is expelled. The bloodstream picks up fresh air and gets rid of waste in an endless cycle. It is an automatic system, but it is up to us to let each breath be free and full.

When breathing is shallow, the body is deprived of the life-giving oxygen it needs for proper functioning, and the toxic waste material is not fully eliminated. What remains in the lungs may re-circulate back through the body. This gradually results in a breakdown of the cells, affecting the brain, the bones, the skin, and every organ in the body, causing disease and premature aging. Practicing deep breathing empties the lungs more completely and allows you to take in more fresh air.

There are many different breathing exercises, each one for a different purpose—to relax, to energize, to cleanse, for meditation, and so on. All are good and helpful, but for now let us just focus on regular everyday breathing.

Begin by noticing whether you are predominantly a chest breather or a belly breather. Place one hand on your lower abdomen, and the other hand on your chest, while you take deep breaths in and out. Notice which hand is moving more than the other. If the upper hand moves more, you are taking only shallow breaths into the upper chest. Most people tend to breathe that way, inhaling into the chest—puffing it out—and collapsing the chest as they exhale. If the hand on your abdomen is moving more it shows you are taking in a good deep breath, one that brings more oxygen into the lower part of the lungs. This is known as an abdominal, or belly breath.

It helps to visualize the diaphragm, a thin dome-shaped muscle that separates the abdomen from the chest cavity. It draws downward as we inhale to allow the lower part of the lungs to fill completely, and moves upward as the air is expelled from the lungs. As the diaphragm expands downward on the inhalation it pushes the abdomen out, and on the exhalation the abdomen comes in and the diaphragm moves upward, pushing the air out. As you practice abdominal breathing, try to notice that action. You will see that only by exhaling completely can you take in enough fresh air. After the exhale your body forces you to inhale, in order to fill the vacuum. That is why I always say breathing out is more important than breathing in.

Practice being a belly breather whenever you think of it, and soon your everyday breathing will improve, as will your general health and state of mind. To maximize your intake of oxygen even more, you may want to practice the complete breath, or three-part breath, as is taught in yoga classes. This exaggerated way of breathing is intended only for exercise purposes. If you want to try it now, first read through the following description, so as to understand what to do before trying to do it.

Notice how you feel before doing this exercise, and again afterward. If you feel dizzy from the increased oxygen, just stop for a few minutes and try again, now or later.

THE COMPLETE BREATH

Sit up straight and get comfortable. Exhale the breath from your lungs.

Then begin the first in-breath by inhaling slowly into the belly through your nose, as if filling up an internal balloon...continuing to inhale into the lower chest... continuing into the upper chest...raising your shoulders slightly so as to fill your lungs completely with oxygen.

To exhale, start by breathing out slowly through pursed lips (like blowing out birthday candles) while dropping the shoulders...emptying the upper chest...then the lower chest...then finally the belly draws in to force out the last bit of the carbon dioxide waste.

At the end of that complete breath, when the lungs are empty, repeat the process: inhale—belly, chest, shoulders...exhale—shoulders, chest, belly. Then do it two more times. Practice daily for maximum benefit.

After a while, abdominal breathing will begin to feel natural. If long-held tension is preventing you from taking a full breath don't get frustrated. That would only cause more tension, and is self-defeating. Whenever you think of it, let your normal relaxed breathing drop down to your abdomen. As an exercise practice, take three or four deep complete breaths every day.

Good breathing is one of the most important keys to good health. It links all aspects of our lives and helps them work together harmoniously. On the physical level, it improves heart rate and blood pressure, relaxes muscles and aids digestion. On the mental level, it quiets the mind and helps us think more clearly and more positively.

Slow breathing can bring negative emotions back to a state of equilibrium and inner peace. In emergencies and other stressful circumstances, breathing deeply and slowly in and out a few times will calm your nerves. In case of a panic attack, blow out as much air as possible, which will force you to inhale. Breathe out through the mouth, breathe in through the nose. Doing that a few times will allow the breath to return to normal. (Seek help if necessary.)

On the spiritual level, breathing links the body to the spirit. The words spirit and breath are often used interchangeably in religious and spiritual writings. (Notice the connection between the words spirit, inspiration and respiration.) Think of how we take a deep breath when inspired by beauty, or encountering wisdom. We gasp in awe at a spectacular scene. We exhale a deep sigh of relief and satisfaction when we feel safe and comfortable. We inflate our chests after a successful accomplishment. These kinds of feelings bring about a healthy state in the body.

When you practice breathing, remember that you are not only taking in oxygen, but also that subtle element known as life force, that feeds the spirit. Of course, the best breathing exercise of all is the one that happens naturally when you sing, dance, laugh and play. And don't forget, if you keep breathing you'll live a long time.

Relaxing through It All

"Stress is the rate of wear and tear on the body."
Hans Selye, M.D.

Problems come in all forms, and if we're not careful they can wear us down. We usually call it stress. But what exactly is stress? When I asked my students for a definition of the word, there were many answers offered—family conflicts, noisy neighbors, money worries and other such disturbances. But I surprised them by saying these are not definitions of stress. Rather, they are *stressors*, situations that can cause us to experience stress…if we let them. When looked at this way, we can see that the discomfort we feel is determined by the way we react to a situation, and for how long we let it disturb us. And this is where we have a choice in the matter.

Hans Selye, M.D., studied the actual biological changes that take place when a person is exposed to stressors. In his book *The Stress of Life,* he describes stress as the degree of damage the body suffers as a result of pain, or emotional disturbances, or ongoing tension. Dr. Selye's work laid the foundation for the field of mind-body health, and introduced the modern concept of stress in humans.

When stressors are continuous and chronic it strains our inner resources, affecting the entire body—interfering with the digestive system, speeding up the heart rate, weakening the immune system and leaving us vulnerable to illness of all kinds. Everyone responds to stress differently. Some will get a stomachache, others a headache, still others will manifest an allergic reaction. Stress will affect whichever area is the most vulnerable. Obviously our bodies have excellent coping mechanisms to counteract negative influences and keep us well, but no matter how great a job they do, we also need to do our part to keep stress under control. We can lessen the amount of destruction to our health and well being by choosing how we respond. We can learn to look at things differently. Countless numbers of my students have said that their lives were changed as a result of learning this important lesson. It certainly has changed mine.

Of course living involves all sorts of disruptive changes, and it would be impossible to live a normal life without some stress. In fact, we don't even want to avoid all stress. That would cut us off from natural human experience. Struggling to achieve a goal, for instance, or intense focus on a creative project, can be stressful, but also positive. The same is true for planning a wedding, or a long trip. As Hans Selye points out, the difference is between stress and distress.

The main thing is not to get too caught up in the disturbing events in our lives. When they occur they naturally affect us, but we can learn to let them go, like the zebra described by Robert Sapolsky, a Stanford University psychologist who has studied wild animals in Africa. In his fascinating book *Why Zebras Don't Get Ulcers*, Sapolsky described a situation where a lion is chasing a zebra. Of course, they are both under extreme stress. The hungry lion is eager to catch his prey and the poor zebra is desperately trying to get away. If the lion wins, he eats, and then he relaxes, and the zebra, of course, has no more problems. If the zebra manages to escape, he very quickly forgets about the attack and returns to grazing, or other zebra activities. His blood pressure returns to normal within minutes, and the harmonious balance of his life systems is restored. He doesn't go and tell his friends, "Guess what just happened to me! It was awful! That lion almost got me!" He doesn't hold on to the fear in his body or in his mind.

As we have learned, the body has a built-in system for survival. In fact, nature actually devised a two-part plan for the protection and survival of our bodies: the long-term survival plan, and the emergency survival plan. These two plans cannot work simultaneously—it's either one or the other.

The long-term plan keeps all systems running smoothly in a state of homeostasis, or harmony, for the sake of growth and development. Minor disturbances are handled quickly by chemical adjustments that are automatically controlled by the brain. In fact, the great and wonderful surprise is that it is a requirement of the long-term survival plan that we feel good, that we feel peaceful and at ease. We are meant to be happy! Or as some say, we are "hard-wired for bliss." In this condition, the whole system whirs smoothly and rapidly, as it should, digesting our food, eliminating toxins, fighting off germs and much more. This is how we stay alive and well.

The emergency plan, on the other hand, is there to jump into action in case of threat to life and limb. In such a case the everyday survival plan can wait, because immediate protection has to come first. Why bother digesting breakfast if we are about to die? If a lion was chasing us for its dinner our brain would instantly activate the "fight or flight" response, which would direct the blood supply away from the digestive system and the immune system, and send it to the arms and legs for extra strength to fight back or get away.

But remember, only one plan can operate at a time, so unless we recover quickly from emergency mode, all the basic life systems will remain curtailed—and that's where the trouble begins. Hopefully, once the danger has passed we would exhale with a big sigh of relief, and like the zebra, the body would return to its normal survival functions of digesting, re-building, and maintaining life. Obviously the emergency sys-tem is meant to be a short-term endeavor. Either you survive the threat and all is well again, in which case normal function-ing resumes, or you don't survive, and it's over.

The emotion of fear is designed to guide us in times of danger, because it reacts instantaneously to protect the body. But the fear reflex is simple-minded. In its zeal to protect us, it reacts to problems large and small as if they were all wild lions, as if run-ning away or fighting back is always the best solution. You can see how damaging it would be for the long-term survival pro-cesses to get disrupted too often, and for too long. The system eventually goes out of whack, leaving every part of the body affected and vulnerable to disease.

Consider the analogy of a firehouse. Normally, when there is no fire, the firefighters carry on their lives, cooking and eat-ing, cleaning and maintaining the trucks and equipment. All is calm and life goes on. Suddenly there is an alarm. Quickly, they gear up for the emergency and rush out to fight the fire. When it is put out they return to the firehouse and resume their rou-tine maintenance jobs. But then suppose there is another alarm and they must rush out again. As soon as they come back there is another alarm, and then another. They become exhausted. They have no chance to recover, to take care of themselves or their equipment. In the same way, when we live under constant stress, our bodies become less equipped to take care of basic maintenance. Unless we take some time each day to relax and recover, we will wear ourselves out before our time.

Think about the stressors in your life and notice your reac-tions to them. How many of those experiences arouse the stress response in you even though they are not actually life threaten-ing. Would it help to fight or run? Can you see that the amount of stress experienced in any situation, even a very intense one, is the result of your reaction to it? What if you simply changed how you look at the situation? It is said that perception is the primary solution to all problems. The slow driver is not trying to aggravate you, but perhaps he is in an unfamiliar neighborhood, trying to find his way. The forgetful waitress may have a sick child at home. Seen in this way, a patient reaction would be more appropriate. Just by looking at a situation from a different perspective it can cease to be a problem, even though nothing has outwardly changed.

The important thing is to become aware of unhealthy stress reactions before they make us sick. Most of us are so used to living with stress that we ignore the messages of pain, discomfort or disease that are asking us to slow down and restore harmony. Instead, we complain about those warning symptoms and take a pill.

Perhaps we can learn to laugh things off as often as possible, and relax. Some people believe they will lose control if they let go of their tension. "Don't tell me to relax," they say, "my tension is the only thing holding me together!" When you learn to relax you become the master of yourself rather than the victim of circumstances. You will have more control than ever in coping with any upsetting situations.

For whatever stressors you have, you can apply the tools and suggestions discussed here. Again, it is the degree of your awareness, and the strength of your intention, that is the "magic" of self-healing. Learn to recognize how you feel when you are not relaxed so you can choose your reaction. The goal is to have as little tension as possible interfering with your good intentions. Your health is in your own hands. Here are two simple practices for achieving deep relaxation. Choose one, and do it either first thing in the morning to start the day off right, or the last thing at night to help you sleep better.

BECOMING HEAVY

Set timer for 10 to 20 minutes. Lie down with a small pillow under your head and a rolled blanket under your knees. Inhale and exhale slowly and evenly for 2 or 3 minutes, then allow breath to return to normal.

Let your jaw go slack and imagine your body becoming heavy like a sandbag. Mentally check your body until every part of you feels heavy. Continue to lie still.

When the timer rings, roll to your side, and arise.

SCANNING THE BODY

Sitting up or lying down, simply notice each part of your body in turn. Allow about 20 to 30 minutes.

Begin by paying attention to your face. Are you frowning, squinting, clenching your jaw or tensing your mouth? If not, recognize that as a good state, as a relaxed state. And if you are, see if they can begin to soften. Allow your eyes to smile gently. Allow a tiny smile to cross your lips. Take a deep slow breath, and exhale.

Put your attention on your neck. Move your head around in all directions, stretching and loosening your neck.

Notice your shoulders and see if they can drop an inch or so. It may help to raise them up to exaggerate the tension, and then just let them drop. Relax for a moment.

Let your arms rest heavily on your lap. (If you are holding this book as you read, rest one arm at a time.) Check for any tension in your hands and fingers. With attention on each finger in turn, they may spontaneously relax.

Slowly move your attention to your chest, stomach, legs and feet, one at a time. Direct it yourself in your own time. And then rest quietly for a few minutes.

Healing Hands

*"The healing touch of acupressure enables
the body to relax deeply."*

Michael Reed Gach

Isn't it great that the simplest and often the most effective solution to pain and discomfort is right at arm's length—our own two hands. Instinctively, we reach for the pain and rub it. It is so simple we hardly think of it as an important means of healing ourselves. It isn't enough to fix a broken bone or heal a serious cut or bruise, but the power of our hands to soothe, comfort, and ease suffering—our own or another's—is profound. The purpose of pain is to warn us, or remind us, of something wrong in the body. It pulls our minds from other concerns and focuses our attention on the place that hurts. It is part of nature's survival system. Automatically, our hands hold and rub and reassure our back, or knee, or whatever hurts, and give it loving care. With that loving attention, the muscle tension around the pain can release, which helps it to heal.

Touch is an ancient form of healing. Animals lick their newborns as a form of massage to promote their development. The loving arms of a mother help the newborn to thrive. In institutions where there is little or no physical contact, babies fail to thrive, and sometimes die, even though they are being fed. The following true story shows the importance of touch.

At a university hospital, a number of rabbits were being studied for the effect of diet on hardening of the arteries. They were kept in cages stacked on a table in a research laboratory and fed high-fat food. When they were tested, fifteen percent of the rabbits were found to have clean arteries. Since this finding made no sense, the study was repeated several times, always with the same results. Finally it was discovered that the student who came in to feed the rabbits was taking those within reach out of their cages to pet them and play with them. These were the rabbits whose arteries were clean.

While the connection between hardening of the arteries and a high-fat diet was the subject of the study, the influence of healing touch altered the expected outcome. Apparently, the loving touch those rabbits received counteracted the stress that the others, isolated and frightened in their cages, experienced. The implication, as reported in the journal *Science,* 1980, is that stress can somehow block the normal assimilation and processing of fat, causing it to build up in the arteries, whereas a positive social environment can enable the body to better deal with high cholesterol foods.

Most traditional cultures use some form of hands-on healing, often in a religious context accompanied by prayer. In modern hospitals, some nurses are using the technique called "therapeutic touch" to help patients recover more quickly from surgery. Therapeutic massage is being offered in various health centers across the country. There are many forms of massage, ranging from gentle but firm stroking, to very strong pressure designed to release long-held muscular tension. Each method is valuable.

Acupressure, Shiatsu, Reiki and Reflexology are some of the hands-on healing systems based on an understanding of the life force energy that flows throughout the body. Ancient Chinese doctors created an elaborate chart outlining the specific pathways along which the energy flows, and the points associated with the various internal organs. Although it is a very complex study, anyone can learn the basic principles of energy medicine and get some benefits. Naturally, a trained professional is best.

In the late seventies I studied with the Japanese Shiatsu master, Reuho Yamada. He lived in San Francisco for a few years, healing and teaching. At the time I had a chronic hip pain that I assumed was due to arthritis, but Reuho told me that Oriental medicine does not use names, such as arthritis, to describe physical problems. Rather, he said, it looks for "energy blocks" or "energy flow." He explained that when the life force energy is blocked from reaching a part of the body, that area begins to malfunction. When the blockage is released, the energy resumes its flow, bringing about a natural healing. When we give an ailment a name, such as arthritis, he said, that fixes it in our bodymind and makes it more difficult to relieve.

Reuho treated the appropriate acupressure points, which got the energy flowing again. Within a few days the pain in my hip disappeared and has never returned. He told me that even without knowing specific pressure points I can take healing into my own hands, literally, by intuitively pressing where I think it will help! I also learned to relax any painful places.

For more specific help with pressure points, I often refer to *Acupressure's Potent Points*, by Michael Reed Gach. His illustrated instructions for using acupressure to relieve many ailments are easy to follow and very useful. Reflexology is a healing system using specific pressure points on the feet and the hands. There are charts available that show where to press to affect different parts of the body. But again, even without knowing the specific points, you can rub and press all over your feet and hands anytime, to great advantage.

Reiki (*rei*-universal, *ki*-energy), which originated in Japan, involves sending healing energy through your hands. You can activate the energy by rubbing your hands together very briskly until they become warm and tingly. Then just rest them lightly on or above any sore place for several minutes. It is easy to do this for yourself or for a friend. As a Reiki healer, I find it effective and powerful. I taught my students to exchange healing touch, and although they had no previous experience, many of them could feel the heat coming from the giver's hands.

What causes the life force to become blocked? Often it is the remains of an old injury, or other trauma to the body, that has caused the muscles to go into spasm. The muscles around the injured area carry a memory of the original pain and are perpetually holding on, in fear of it happening again. This is where healing touch comes in. Gentle self-massage can convince the frightened cells and muscles that they are safe. They figuratively give a sigh of relief, and let go. Try this simple treatment.

SELF-MASSAGE

Remove constricting shoes or clothing. Sit comfortably.

Breathe deeply in and out, exhaling with a releasing sigh.

Press firmly with your fingers all over your head and face.

Press the back of your neck and under the scalp.

Massage one shoulder at a time with the opposite hand.

Rub and press all over each arm from shoulder down to wrists, feeling the muscles.

Rub and massage each finger and your whole hand.

Rub your belly gently, all over.

Press and squeeze your thigh muscles, and down your legs.

Rub and massage your feet all over.

Take a few minutes to relax and notice how you feel. If there is serious pain, you can stroke the painful area gently, or just lightly rest your hands on (or above) the area to provide warmth and comfort. If it seems to help, continue the massage for at least five to ten minutes until you start to feel better. Repeat it whenever pain returns. If there is no improvement soon, or if the pain gets too severe, be sure to get help. On the other hand, if your condition improves, give thanks, and acknowledge your natural built-in healing abilities.

Even when there is no pain or injury you may want to give yourself the gift of self-massage at the end of a busy day.

Part Two

Mind

It's All In Your Mind

"You can't afford the luxury of a negative thought."
Unknown

Have you ever been told your pains or complaints were all in your mind? Most of us have at one time or another, and of course it made us feel worse. Nobody listened to us, and the pain continued. Well I hate to say it, but those unsympathetic people were right, to some degree. As the study of the mind-body connection has shown, our physical problems are reactions to the negative quality of our thinking. When we have physical complaints we might want to look for the thoughts that preceded them. Have you been calling someone "a pain in the neck?" Such thoughts can manifest in the body.

Thoughts are real—real enough to cause a lot of damage or a lot of joy. A thought can give you goose flesh or make you smile, make your fists tighten, or lead to a nice deep breath and a sigh, and cause you to relax. Of course the mind and body are connected!

In research studies where patients are given a placebo (dummy medication), believing it is real, their bodies often produce the same chemical changes as if the medicine were real. Sometimes a placebo can bring about a complete cure. For years scientists considered this a meaningless coincidence. Now it is being recognized as an example of the mind-body connection.

Try this experiment to see how a thought and a mental image can cause an automatic physical response.

LEMON EXPERIMENT

Imagine a bowl of lemons in your kitchen... Take one in your hand and feel the bumpy yellow skin... Bring it to your nose and smell the lemony smell... Now, picture yourself slowly cutting the lemon in half with a sharp knife... Watch the juice drip out onto the counter...Imagine tasting a drop of the sour juice... Now, stop and notice whether extra saliva is forming in your mouth simply as a result of using your imagination.

The role of the mind is to assess what it perceives, and to send an appropriate message to the body about how to react. Is a particular situation threatening, or simply challenging? If the mind is not paying attention it might send a "mindless" message, causing the body to react inappropriately. This is a key to mind-body healing—while the body has its built-in survival mechanism to deal with stresses of all kinds, it is up to the mind to interpret degrees of danger and adjust the stress response accordingly. In the case of sudden danger, such as a near accident, the body's emergency system takes over, responding more quickly than the mind could.

If thoughts have actual physical consequences, it behooves us to be careful about what we think. But is it possible to change our thoughts? They seem so out of control sometimes. Most people's minds run constantly, like a television set with a broken switch and no way to turn it off. They go on planning the future, or regretting the past, or worrying about everything in between. That makes it almost impossible to stop and choose the most appropriate response to what is happening in the moment. Mind-body medicine teaches our minds to be the captain of the ship. This will be discussed more later, but first we have to learn which thoughts will get us to where we want to be, and which ones will not.

One of the traps some people get into is what has been called "awfulizing." You expect the worst possible thing to happen and you go over and over it in your mind, or out loud to others. "Oh, it will be so awful," you exclaim. I have done my share of awfulizing, but it made me suffer as much as if the situation had already occurred. Why expect the worst, when it could just as easily turn out to be the best? What a waste of suffering. What a waste of time. Meanwhile I can live in the present moment, enjoying my life and using a positive frame of mind to imagine, and aim for, the best possible outcome.

Judgmental thoughts are also stressful to the body and do us no good. Whether we are judging ourselves, or others, we are allowing negative thinking to create disharmony in our bodies. Many of the things that upset us are trivial, yet we often feel compelled to hold on to them just to prove a point. Letting go, when appropriate, is good for the mind and body.

Certainly we want to examine all possible eventualities so as to make intelligent decisions, but once in a while we have to slow down all the thinking and mental activity. With a quiet mind we can step outside of the situation and take stock of what is really happening. Then we can make choices. Even if things do not turn out as we would like, we can choose to have a philosophical attitude and assume it is all for the best in the long run. Reflecting back, we may recall other difficult situations that turned out better than expected.

It takes intelligence and determination to choose which kinds of thoughts we allow to occupy our minds. And it takes practice. But the harm of leaving thoughts unchecked is well known. We attract to ourselves what we focus on, whether it is what we want or what we don't want. That is why it is so important to be clear about what we want to attract, and dismiss from our minds what we don't. It is a skill that takes practice. But we simply can't afford the "luxury" of thinking negative thoughts.

What You Say Matters

"Every day, in every way, I'm getting better and better."
Emil Coué

Years ago I taught my children to say the well-known rhyme about getting better and better, when they were sick. It came from Emil Coué, a French physician in the early 1900s, who taught the power of positive words in his book *Self-Mastery through Conscious Auto-Suggestion.* Although we thought it was a little silly, we repeated those words over and over. I also learned to say "Everything is all right!" when times were tough, and it seemed to help. I admit that many times I forgot to be positive, and I complained about how things are getting worse and worse.

Often we unconsciously repeat certain negative words and phrases in our minds. Sometimes we repeat the same words throughout our lives. They are part of us. They are part of our history. We have been told these things from early on and believed them, and we continue to act them out. We call our-selves lazy and worthless and expect that we will never amount to anything. We are sure we will die young because our grand-father did. These habitual beliefs that stick in our heads, left over from parents and teachers and society in general, affect how we think, what we expect, and how much we worry, or don't. They affect how we take care of ourselves, and how soon we give up trying.

The study of the mind-body connection has not only shown

that the words we say and think have the power to change our lives, but also that we have the power to change the words we use. We can speak to ourselves with encouraging words instead of discouraging ones. We can expect the best, look at the bright side, see the cup as half full instead of half empty.

A repeated positive statement is called an affirmation. It says that something is so, or made firm. When we state something with conviction, the bodymind picks up the message and begins acting as if it were already true. Affirmations have helped many people accomplish their goals, but often we repeat statements that are not very positive. Not being aware of the power of our thoughts, we express our fears and self-doubt instead: "I'll never get that job." "I'm getting sick." Become aware of those negative affirmations going around in your head. When you notice such words try to reverse them: "I have a wonderful new job!" "I take good care of myself and I feel great." Or, "My body's own internal healing system is eliminating all destructive germs and viruses, and I am healthy and well." Indeed, our healing system and all the body's cells are listening in and responding to our thoughts.

Saying affirmations is something like changing a computer program that isn't working for you. As they say in computer-ese, "garbage in, garbage out." So if some of the thoughts going around in your head sound like garbage, reprogram, or actually rewrite, the story of who you are, such as, "I am successful in reaching my goals." Say what you sincerely want to be, not what you think you are! State it positively and in the present tense. Our words and thoughts can influence any area of life we choose to focus on.

The change you want may not happen as soon as you expect or hope it will. There is no established timeline by which to judge success. But you can try to refine your words and thoughts and pay attention to how you are stating your affirmations. This is somewhat tricky. For example, if you say, "I need a new job," you are focusing on the need. The message you are sending out expresses your feeling of lack. Whereas an affirmation says it is already true: "I have a wonderful new job." Remember, we want to say it as if it is already done, and it helps to think about how good it feels to have that wonderful job.

It is best to repeat your affirmations several times a day, aloud or silently, while focusing on the meaning of the words. If you want to use affirmations most effectively, it is best to have an attitude of positive expectation. Like a child, your body will respond to congratulations: "You're doing great!" "Good work!"

One of the best sources I know for learning how to use affirmations is Louise Hay's classic book *Heal Your Body*. She has taught hundreds of thousands of people to recognize the mental and emotional causes of physical illness. Her book is a quick reference guide to many different physical ailments with suggested affirmations to heal them.

Taking some time to learn to think differently is a route to changing how you deal with life. It is not dishonest to change how you think, to say new words, and react in new ways. Since the future doesn't yet exist, it is not truer to expect the worst than the best. Positive benevolent thoughts harm no one. If the old ways aren't serving you, try new ways.

Learning to use the power of the mind requires, first of all, a strong desire to change. Be very clear about what you want to change, and why. Examine options and resources so as to make intelligent choices. Then keep your thoughts focused on this new vision of yourself and your life situation. When your mind strays into the swamp of negative thinking simply notice it without judgment, and then bring it back. You may have to do this many times before it becomes second nature to keep your attention mostly on positive thoughts.

Fear of failure and fear of disappointment prevent some people from practicing affirmations. Of course there is no guarantee of success in any kind of healing practice, and we may never know why we got better or why we didn't. Giving it our best effort is all we can do. Being skeptical is understandable, but not helpful, since it interferes with positive expectation.

Changing your thinking is not an easy thing to do. Sometimes you don't even know what you think or what you want! It takes time to convince your bodymind of your new beliefs. After all, a lifetime of habitual thinking led you to where you are. To make changes also could take some time—hopefully not as long. Medical science is only just beginning to explore the power of thoughts to change the physical body—but why wait? Try it and see for yourself.

Affirmations are personal. You may hear one you particularly like and want to adopt for yourself, or you can make one up to suit your own specific needs. Think about your goals. What is it you want to change? What do you want to accomplish? When you are clear about what you want, write it down in simple strong words as if it is already so, and repeat it throughout the day whenever you think of it. Don't be afraid to say what you really want. But remember to be careful about what you ask for because, as they say, you might get it. If your goal is a better job, for instance, are you ready for the extra responsibility and longer hours it might entail?

What I am describing is a self-healing tool to use only for yourself. It should never be used for trying to change another person. Some people like to write down their affirmations artistically and then hang them someplace where they will see them throughout the day and be reminded. Or you can cut out words and pictures from magazines that reflect your dreams. Use your imagination. Have fun with it.

ᴀ Picture Is Worth a Thousand Pills

*"Imagery is the natural way the body stores
and processes information."*
Martin Rossman, M.D.

Most children live in their imaginations, creating cities of building blocks or whole scenarios acted out with dolls or tiny toy soldiers. It is the way children learn. But as we get older we are told to get serious, be realistic, stop making believe and grow up. We learn not to trust our ability to imagine because our dreams may seem unreasonable or impossible. Yet it is the creative thinkers and inventors who influence the world the most. They can imagine something new and make it happen.

Everyone pictures things all the time, often randomly, but when used intentionally, "imagery" can be a powerful force to heal the body or to create other changes in our lives. Martin Rossman, M.D., physician and acupuncturist, is a pioneer in using imagery in his practice in Sausalito, California. His book *Healing Yourself with Mental Imagery,* includes imagery scripts you can use for various purposes.

Another book of scripts you can read to yourself, or to someone else, is *Rituals of Healing: Using Imagery for Health and Wellness,* by Barbara Dossey, R.N., Jeanne Achterberg, Ph.D., and Leslie Kolkmeier, R.N. These can be very helpful in many cases.

Just as watching a movie can cause the palms to sweat, the heart to race or tears to flow, even though it isn't real, the pictures that come into our minds can also cause either negative or positive physical effects. Why not use imagery intentionally as a tool for relaxing, for healing specific ailments, or perhaps for overcoming unwanted habits. You can create a new mental movie, a new script.

Our thoughts and imagination affect us all the time in subtle ways, whether we know it or not. It makes sense to take control of those wayward minds of ours. After all, who is in charge here anyway? Did the captain of this ship fall asleep on the job, and allow it to go off course? The beauty of the practice of self-healing is the power it gives us to take control simply by becoming aware that we have that power. But don't forget, when you have the power, you also have the responsibility. Make sure your mental images, like your words, are acting in your favor, and not against your best interests—or anyone else's.

Will you imagine something peaceful, to send a message of relaxation to your body? Or will you imagine disaster, and prepare for battle, which will take a toll on your body? And haven't you noticed that most of your tension comes from imagining the worst, rather than from actual things or events? As Dr. Rossman said, "We have to stop scaring ourselves to death."

As a healing practice, imagery is increasingly being used in some hospitals along with other mind-body treatments. The images you use don't need to be physically accurate or realistic. They are only meant to stimulate your healing response, and it seems that fantasy works just as well.

Patients may be asked to think of an image that describes their pain. Have you ever had a "knot" in your shoulder? Picture an actual knot in your shoulder or back and then imagine slowly untying it. As you visualize the loosening of a knotted rope, your knotted muscles are subconsciously induced to loosen as well. Or, if the pain is described as sharp, as if from a knife, you could create a clear image in your mind of slowly drawing out the knife. For a burning pain, you could apply an imaginary icy glove to the area, or plunge it into snow. You could also try turning down the pain volume on your special imaginary remote control. Imagery techniques such as these are helping many people alleviate their pain enough to live normal lives.

Athletes often use imagery to improve their performance by practicing their sport mentally. Visualizing the perfect golf stroke, or tennis serve, or other action, can teach the body to act accordingly, improving even without actual practice! One woman practiced T'ai Chi Chih in a hospital bed, to great advantage. This has enormous implications. Imagery can potentially be used as a tool for increased performance in many areas.

Several years ago I had a good lesson in imagery from one of my students. The day before, as I was walking in the park, I was knocked down by a large dog that accidentally ran into me from behind, causing me to land hard, flat on my back. It was quite a jolt, but soon I was able to get up and go on my way. In class that next day, my neck was hurting and I mentioned that I had taken a hard fall. At that, a student suggested that by saying I fell down "hard" I was reinforcing the trauma in my mind, and therefore in my body. She suggested I say I fell like "gelatin." As she said the word, I visualized the soft bounciness of gelatin. My whole body armor softened, and very soon my pain disappeared completely. This young student had learned about the mind-body connection from her parents, who were both medical doctors in Brazil. I was reminded again of the power of a word.

Healing with the imagination probably sounds impossible, until we realize how natural it is to picture things, and how simply the body responds to these pictures. If, as Dr. Rossman says, we store and process our experiences in the brain and nervous system with imagery, then we can use imagery to experience them differently. Will you picture the worst, or envision your hopes and dreams? Will you see yourself as ailing, or well?

The following guided imagery practice can help you create a special imaginary place where you may feel very relaxed. After reading it over a few times you will probably be able to make up your own script. Or record it so you can play it back.

GUIDED IMAGERY

Sit in a quiet place and get comfortable. Then read the following script, stopping for a moment after each suggestion.

Imagine a place where you feel totally relaxed and comfortable... it could be a place where you have been before, or a place where you would like to be. (Take a moment to decide on a place, then don't change it.) Visualize a scene that is very pleasing to you, and as well as you can, try to picture the surroundings.

Read slowly now, or close your eyes, as you imagine where this place is and what it looks like. Maybe it is a quiet beach house, or a cabin in the woods, or your grandmother's porch... It could be someplace you have read about... or a scene you dream up... If you have difficulty imagining a place, think of your own room... The important thing is that you feel very peaceful and comfortable there.

If you like, find a place to sit down. It could be on the grass, or a sandy beach, or in a comfortable chair... Slowly look around... Smell the air and feel the warm sun, or perhaps a gentle breeze.

When you feel very relaxed and comfortable you may want to ask a question about your health or other situation... Wait and see what comes into your mind... If nothing does, make it up. Use your imagination. Or, simply relax in this special place for as long as you like, feeling peaceful and comfortable. When you are ready to return, take a deep breath and exhale slowly.

Sit quietly for a while to enjoy the relaxed feeling you may be experiencing. If any interesting thoughts or images come up, pay attention to them and perhaps write them down. They may offer clues that answer questions you have about your health. This healing place is always available, and you can visit it anytime.

Healing techniques such as affirmations and guided imagery are effective tools for replacing negative thoughts with positive ones. They can help us return to our natural state of relaxation and harmony.

Intention: It All Starts Here

"Intention is the healing elixir."

Unknown

We can begin to take charge of our health by becoming aware of our unhealthy behavior patterns. But to really bring about change, we need something more. We need a good strong intention—a decision that focuses and directs the necessary attention to get things done. Setting an intention clarifies our goals and organizes our thinking. It offers a chance to consider consequences and alternatives before deciding to act. Without intention, changing is haphazard. One day we think about it, the next day we forget. Sound familiar? Before we do anything, whether it's to go for a walk or build a house, cook a meal or write a book, first we decide—we have an intention. Practicing self-healing is the same.

We're all good at writing New Years resolutions, but when we fail to follow through we say we have no willpower, and we give up. Yet sticking to our good intentions, whether at the New Year or any other time of year, is not about willpower or self-discipline, it is about having a very strong desire, a clear goal, and a realistic strategy for accomplishing it. As Dr. Phil McGraw, the popular television psychologist, tells us, "Goals are dreams with a timeline and accountability." If we are serious about our intention to live a healthier life we will make some decisions and be accountable to ourselves. It is like going to college—once you sign up for a course you do whatever the assignment requires to the best of your ability. In taking responsibility for your health you set the course for yourself, and assess your own results.

The first step is to ask yourself what you really want and why you want it? What benefits will come from achieving it? Is it important enough to make sacrifices for? What are the obstacles? Reflecting on these questions will help you to clarify your position about what course to follow.

Then you have to decide whether you are ready to move in the direction of your choice—to believe in it and to work toward it. Making this conscious decision is important, otherwise the tendency to forget, to resist, or to get distracted, interferes with your goal. Of course, you don't have to sign up.

When I need to give my health a boost I state my intention, or decision, to think and talk about what I want to experience instead of what I dread, and I hold an image of that in my mind. I intend to maintain a state of relaxation as much as possible and avoid letting little things bother me. I intend to eat according to my self-chosen plan and to exercise according to my ability. I will take time to aim toward my goal every day in some way, and I will not feel like a failure if I slack off occasionally. And lastly, if I feel I need help in sticking to my intentions I will seek it in the form of counseling, or a support group, or by talking with a good friend.

After the intention comes the next step—attention. Paying attention is the commitment to persevere in your self-healing work whether or not results are immediately apparent. Keeping your attention on your plan involves practicing everyday like a professional athlete or dancer, rain or shine, even if you don't feel like doing it. If forever seems too long to stick to a health plan, set a timeline that is logical for your specific goal and make a decision to stick to that. Picture what you want, and imagine how you will feel when you have achieved it. Hold that vision in spite of obstacles or setbacks. Every morning, take a moment to state your intention for that day to go smoothly, and for your plans to be accomplished successfully. Practice by intending small things at first.

Feeling guilty about your faults, and hopeless about your ability to change, is the greatest deterrent to self-improvement. None of us is perfect, but with a little willingness you can take the first steps. Do you doubt that you can control your health in the ways I have suggested? Do you feel powerless to change? What forces in your life led to those feelings? Perhaps you are not as powerless as you have been led to believe you are.

The first thing that motivates change is knowing we have options. And when we really understand how change would improve our lives, we are more likely to make the necessary effort. Actually, trying something new is the only way to find out what will bring the effect we want, so it is wise to take an experimental approach. As they say, if you keep on doing what you're doing, you'll keep on getting what you've got!

What happens to your mood when you start each day with five slow deep breaths? How do you feel when you drink more water? Look over some of the points in this book and let them help you to set your intention. When you discover what makes you feel better, it may encourage you to continue. Begin your self-healing program whenever you are ready—or not at all. It's your choice.

For many years I was my own little research lab. But I admit my science was pretty sloppy. I would try something for a week, then seeing no immediate results I would give up and start another "miracle" regimen. After a while I boiled down my understanding to some basic principles, and once my intentions were clear my efforts were more successful.

Being Mindful

"Don't just do something, sit there."

Jon Kabat-Zinn

If you find yourself running around from one activity or task to another and missing out on today, I urge you to make a point of stopping. Give yourself a break once in a while. Allow time to just sit quietly alone, watching your breath go in and out, and observing your thoughts flowing through your open mind. Thich Nhat Hanh, the Vietnamese Buddhist monk, says, "All your life you have been running. Practice stopping." Why not set an intention to stop and do nothing for just five or ten minutes a day with no expectations and no guilt?

Taking the time to be entirely with yourself rather than looking for something or someone outside, is a form of self-respect. It is a way to get in touch with a quiet place inside that usually goes unnoticed. Maybe it is the wise part. Maybe it has the answers we have been looking for. It may take a while to learn to stop our overactive minds, but soon the muddy waters of the mind will settle and we will become calmer, more focused and more aware, bringing harmony to body, mind and spirit.

When I was a child I would often gaze absent-mindedly out the window. My mother, an artist with several creative projects going all the time, would tell me to stop daydreaming and do something constructive. Now I am trying to replace her message with Jon Kabat-Zinn's message, from his book *Wherever You Go, There You Are,* and stop doing so much.

Many of us judge ourselves for being forgetful, or careless, or thoughtless. Perhaps we are simply overwhelmed by the pressures of life and the problems of the world. Perhaps we are always thinking thinking thinking, and not paying attention to our surroundings. The trouble is, if our mind is off somewhere worrying about the future or regretting the past, we might not notice the crack in the sidewalk, or the speeding car. When we forget where we put the keys, are we blaming it on getting old? Or is it just a habit of mindlessness?

Becoming mindful takes practice. It is the practice of paying full attention to whatever is going on around us at the time. The Buddhist practice of "mindfulness meditation" trains us to bring awareness into everyday life situations. Here is a simple version of that meditation exercise. As always, it requires choosing an appropriate time when you won't be interrupted, sitting still, and becoming as comfortable and relaxed as you can. Your eyes may be closed or open.

MINDFULNESS MEDITATION

First, notice your breath as it flows in and out of your nostrils...notice the coolness of the air as it enters your nose...then notice that the air is slightly warmer as it flows out. Take a few minutes to be very mindful of the action of the breath in...and...out.

Notice any distracting thoughts that come into your mind, without trying to stop them...just notice the act of thinking...no need to be attached to them. When your mind wanders...watch the thoughts as they float into and out of your mind...like leaves floating down a river, or like clouds passing by. Whether they are good thoughts or disturbing ones...simple observe them, and then let them go.

Next, become tuned in to the sense of hearing...not what you are hearing, but hearing itself. Just become aware of any sounds, whether close by or in the distance. If there is no sound at all, notice that. Spend a few minutes focusing your attention on the act of hearing.

Allow your attention to rest on any feelings of discomfort in your body. Nothing is good or bad, just recognize where you feel uncomfortable.

Become mindful of the sense of touch...the contact of your body against the chair...the feeling of your clothing on your body...your feet in your shoes...your shoes against the floor...your hands in your lap. Just recognize each impression, one at a time, and then let it go.

Take your time becoming mindful of your senses and your feelings.

Now, open your eyes and experience the sense of seeing...just gaze at your surroundings without looking at any particular thing...just notice the act of seeing.

In time, practicing mindfulness meditation will help your mind to become more centered, rather than scattered, so you can focus on your goals. You will do whatever it is you do—walk, drive, cook, eat, or anything else—with full attention.

58   The Healer is You

Part Three

Emotions

Feelings? What Are Those?

*"The body and mind are one system coordinated
by the molecules of emotion."*

Candace Pert, Ph. D.

The next aspect of who we are is our feelings, or emotions. But what are they? Are they physical, or are they mental, or both, or neither? What purpose do they have, or is there any purpose to them at all? How do they affect our lives? What do they have to do with health? Do we have any control over them, or do they control us? In this book about self-healing we cannot avoid talking about the emotions, one of the most important keys to health and happiness.

Emotions are physical reactions to how the senses perceive outside circumstances. Our senses of seeing, smelling, hearing, touching and tasting give us the experience of our surroundings, and send appropriate messages to the brain. If something beautiful and inspiring such as a waterfall or a sunset arouses our senses, there is a physical reaction of elation. Take a moment to imagine what that would feel like in your shoulders, and in your face.

What about the effect of disturbing events, such as a sudden noise in the house at night, or the loss of something important, or an insult from a co-worker or a neighbor. Each of these situations could cause physical tension. Pause for a few minutes and try to imagine the feeling of adrenaline flowing throughout your body trying to deal with a perceived threat. Fear might make your arms and legs become tense—preparing to fight or flee. An insult might cause tightness in your chest, fast breathing, a red face, heart palpitations, or perspiration. These are normal reactions to how we think about, and more importantly how we interpret, what happens to us. It appears to be automatic—an insult leads to hurt feelings, which leads to bodily tension, whereas a compliment creates happy feelings that lead to relaxation. However, you have more power over your emotions than you might think.

During this natural process of perception leading to a reaction, the mind, as we discussed earlier, actually has the ability to choose how to interpret the experience, and thus how to react. What if you quickly realized that the sound in the night was only the screen door banging? You were frightened—but then you relaxed. The insult from your neighbor was hurtful—but when you considered her point of view you understood, and then you were able to let it go and you felt relieved. In each case, your physical reaction changed when you thought about the situation from a different perspective.

I suggest that health is not just freedom from physical symptoms, but freedom from the kinds of reactions to events in life that wear on the body's systems. The respiratory system, especially, is affected by our negative emotions. Notice that when we're angry we tend to huff and puff—stronger exhalation. Sadness makes us sob—mostly inhalation. Fear causes us to hold our breath—little breath at all. And the whole body suffers.

Candace Pert, Ph.D., pharmacologist and biochemist formerly with the National Institutes of Health, discovered the biochemical basis of the mind-body connection. In her book *The Molecules of Emotion,* she describes her discoveries in the laboratory that demonstrate how thoughts and feelings affect physical health. She explains that "the body and mind are one intelligent system that constantly sends chemical messages, called neurotransmitters, back and forth through a network that reacts automatically to signals from our thoughts and feelings." Her work clearly shows the importance of being mindful of what we think and feel.

Emotions are normal and necessary for the protection of the body, and as a way to better understand ourselves. Their messages may guide us to go in a new direction, or to change our attitude. Rather than denying our feelings, it is important to pay attention to them and learn from them.

In this chapter, we will try to understand and recognize our emotions, and by looking at them honestly, manage them. Positive emotions such as love and happiness, peacefulness and contentment, are not too difficult to recognize. But understandably, we tend to want to hide from the painful ones. That is how they become a problem. By suppressing or ignoring unpleasant feelings we allow disharmony to pervade the bodymind network, creating ongoing stress that weakens the body.

How do you feel right now? Take a moment to see if you can name the feeling you are experiencing. Most of us have not been taught to notice what we are feeling. Instead we get lost in the feeling without paying attention to what it is, how it feels, and what it is telling us. Recognizing our emotions is the first step in learning to deal with them. Of course, feelings can change from day to day and moment by moment, and these can be observed as they occur. But other feelings have been with us for so long we don't even notice them.

Take a few moments to glance over this list of negative emotions to see if any of them apply. You might want to write those down. Of course, this is purely voluntary. It is a natural tendency to want to push unpleasant feelings out of our minds, yet to do so allows them to continue affecting our lives.

NEGATIVE EMOTIONS

anger	shame	boredom
confusion	depression	jealousy
anxiety	resentment	frustration
sadness	helplessness	guilt
hurt	insecurity	worry

Although each emotion feels different from the others, all negative emotions are rooted in fear, often as a result of childhood experiences. People who grow up feeling weak and helpless may be afraid of life. Some, due to shame or guilt, live in fear of being discovered to be bad or wrong. Others are afraid to trust, always expecting someone to take advantage of them. They are suspicious and resentful. The fear of abandonment is often the source of feelings of insecurity, betrayal, or jealousy. The fear of failure is very real for some people, while others fear too much success, inwardly believing they don't deserve it.

Large numbers of people live with a general unfocused anxiety resulting from money worries, health worries, loneliness, or fear of the unknown future. Whether we are feeling personally inadequate, or feeling threatened by conditions in our community or in the world, the fact is that many people don't feel happy and don't feel safe. In extreme cases, these kinds of feelings can lead to dangerous behavior such as drug addiction, crime, or suicide. When we realize the degree of desperation some people are experiencing, it sheds some light on the causes of violence in the world.

Many people avoid facing their fears and troubles by constantly watching television, or doing anything that will keep their minds occupied. Some escape into their work, and may even become very successful due to their diligence. They hide their feelings from themselves, or ignore them, thinking they will go away and be forgotten. In the process, they often stop feeling altogether. "I'm strong," they say, "I have no problems. That's for weaklings. Feelings? Feelings? What are those?" It seems safer to live on the surface of life and not dig too deeply.

I once got a thorn in the side of my foot that I couldn't remove. After a while it stopped hurting so I ignored it. I didn't want to deal with it. It healed over and I almost forgot about it until about a year later, when it began to fester. Finally it pushed its way to the surface, forcing me to pay attention to it by becoming inflamed and painful. After I took care of it my foot was able to heal. Buried emotions, like the thorn, also need to be removed so we can live without the underlying discomfort they cause.

Dealing with the struggles of life can be very challenging, but as hard as it is to face our deepest fears, it is probably worse to keep them hidden. Regardless of the cause of the problem, facing and understanding the emotional source gives us some control, and offers a path to healing.

Christiane Northrup, M.D., gynecologist/obstetrician and author of *Women's Bodies, Women's Wisdom*, discusses the danger of not dealing with negative emotions. She explains that if these feelings are not worked through and released they can get trapped in the body and become toxic. Fear, guilt and resentment are like poison to the body. Some doctors consider them to be a medical risk as severe as smoking. As with other health risks, the damage builds up over the years and gradually, without our awareness, diminishes our health and shortens our lives.

Louise Hay, herself a survivor of cancer, says, "Cancer comes from a pattern of deep resentment that is held for a long time until it literally eats away at the body." With the help of her healers and teachers, she came to terms with the trauma she experienced as a child. By changing her thoughts and forgiving her abusers, her internal healing system was able to ward off the disease. While genetic and environmental factors are known to cause cancer, emotional issues may interfere with the will to live, affecting the body's ability to fight it off.

Emotional pain is nothing to be ashamed of. It means something has gone wrong and needs attention in the same way that physical pain indicates a disorder in the body that needs care. Instead of looking away and ignoring that pain, we need to give it our most tender, loving care. We can become the devoted parent, or caregiver, to our own emotional suffering. We can reassure that frightened child inside of us that it is safe to feel our feelings again.

Emotional health is related to love—the natural, harmonious state. And as we have shown, all negative emotions are rooted in some form of fear. If love is our true nature, then fear must be a mistake—an obstruction of who we really are. When fear is removed, love remains.

Remember the Child Within

"Begin slowly to allow the memories to come up and out."
Eliana Gil, Ph.D.

 $\mathcal{E}$ very one of us came into this world pure and innocent, deserving to be accepted and protected. That consistent sense of safety and reassurance paves the way for the bodymind system to develop harmoniously. Jean Liedloff, in her classic book, *The Continuum Concept,* tells about her experience of living with a tribe of Stone Age Indians in the Amazon jungle for more than two years. She noticed how much happier they were than the average Americans she knew, and wondered why. Over time she observed that each baby was completely welcomed and comforted from the moment of birth. And she was impressed with the respectful way the young children were corrected and guided as they grew up. Witnessing the kindness and joyfulness in the way these "uncivilized" people treated each other, she attributed it to how they had been raised.

As a result of her experiences, Jean Liedloff had the realization that it is the evolutionary expectation of the newborn of every species to come into the world with complete acceptance and approval and close physical contact. This is nature's design for survival, a "continuum" of the basic emotional requirements for a good healthy life passed down to the off-spring of each generation.

La Leche League International, an organization dedicated to "good mothering through breastfeeding," teaches a philosophy very much in line with Jean Liedloff's recommendations, as described in *The Continuum Concept*. (In the mid-sixties, I was a group leader and counselor for La Leche League. They continue to offer free support groups and information for mothers in most cities in the U.S. and around the world.)

Jean Liedloff recognized that individuals deprived of these biologically programmed requirements must forever seek to fulfill them. This may cause them to feel unlovable, and then to behave as if they were bad, clumsy and stupid. They have an innate need to regain the basic sense of security and self-worth that never had a chance to develop normally. In some cases their survival system may become unbalanced, and eventually goes haywire. Some deprived children grow up feeling cheated and resentful. To them the world is a dangerous place and they are forever insecure and nervous.

Lacking that basic sense of "rightness," as Liedloff described it, these individuals may succumb to self-destructive activities and addictions such as alcohol and drug abuse, violent behavior, sexual addiction, or over-eating, in a futile attempt to feel right, or in other words—relaxed. If this theory is correct, then depriving children of their sense of rightness could be the cause of all the world's problems! Children whose essential needs are met from birth are calm and happy. They have no need to harm themselves or anyone else.

Joseph Chilton Pearce supports this theory in *Magical Child*, and *Magical Child Matures*. He explains that children need consistent quality care at every stage of their development. That gives them the security to progress to each successive stage. If the requirements of each stage are not fully satisfied children can remain emotionally stuck, to some extent, even while physically advancing to the next level. Although they may grow up to be capable and responsible adults, the gaps in their development could lead to unexplained negative emotions and dysfunctional behavior.

From this perspective, it seems that very few of us are perfectly whole with no gaps, and some degree of stress and unhappiness is the inevitable result. No one can really be blamed for this sad situation. It begins with parents who may never have received their own biologically required sense of acceptance, reassurance and approval. How can they provide security for their children when they don't feel safe and strong themselves? The conflict between the unfulfilled needs of parents and the needs and demands of children, makes parenting very difficult and can lead to all forms of abuse. Unwanted children, born to people emotionally unprepared to care for them, are likely to experience neglect, violence, or exploitation. And the cycle goes on and on.

Child sexual abuse is called a "secret syndrome." Due to guilt, shame and intimidation, children are often unable to tell anyone what is happening, yet the effects can be very traumatic. Children should be encouraged to talk about their feelings, and they should be believed. Secrecy is the factor that allows it to continue. Therefore talking about it, and uncovering the secret, is the primary solution to the problem. Understand that it is never the fault of the abused child. Anyone who takes advantage of a child is solely responsible.

Eliana Gil, Ph.D, in her clear and sensitive little book, *Outgrowing the Pain: A Book for and about Adults Abused as Children*, advises these adults to gradually allow the memories to come up and out, so they can be healed.

Fortunately the cycle can be broken. Recognizing it, and realizing the source of the problem, is the first step to healing. It is evident that many adults who were abused as children have broken the destructive cycle and have become excellent people and wonderful parents. Having at least one supportive person in their life, and other favorable factors, can counteract some of the harmful effects.

In *Thou Shalt Not Be Aware: Society's Betrayal of the Child*, Swiss psychoanalyst Alice Miller explains that most psychological problems are "normal reactions to abnormal experiences." Rather than being labeled neurotic, or sick, or bad, these behaviors can be seen as coping mechanisms by which people try to adapt to traumatic events in their past.

Lacking support and understanding, early trauma shocks the system into a fear/stress response that persists. It can leave people with an irrational fear of imminent danger, a feeling of inferiority, or a sense of worthlessness. They may feel they can never fully relax or trust. As adults, the trauma remains locked in memory and in the very cells of the body. The cause of the body's protective holding may be forgotten, but the muscles cannot let go. Chronic fear sets off continuous warning signals to the body cells as if there is an emergency, exhausting the protection system. Bells and sirens are going off in the mind. The fight or flight response is activated, but there is no one to fight and nothing to run from. Trauma is the ultimate stress, which is why in order to live a fully healthy life it must be addressed.

School can be abusive in its own way. While most children seem to thrive in school, others are being traumatized by their school experiences, which can destroy their self-confidence and their love of learning. Teaching methods based on competition, threats and punishment create fear and anxiety in children, and is a major cause of toxic shame. For children who do not respond well to these commonly accepted practices school can have long-lasting emotional and/or physical consequences. When they grow up the source of the fears may be forgotten, but the feelings of unworthiness may remain deep inside.

Dorothy was a small woman in her eighties who attended my

classes in San Francisco. She walked with little mincing steps. During a discussion in class about the effect of early traumatic experiences she suddenly recalled an incident from her childhood. As a little girl in first grade her feet didn't reach the floor when she sat at her desk. Her teacher had put a little box there to rest her feet on, but sometimes she kicked it accidentally, making a loud clatter. For that the teacher punished her by keeping her in at recess. Recalling this humiliation, and telling her story, apparently released the chronic ache in both of her shins, and a few weeks later she told the class that the pain was gone.

Although Dorothy had forgotten, until then, the incident that caused her legs to hurt, her body had remembered the fear and the shame. Hopefully, by tracing back these kinds of memories and understanding how they affect our lives, it might be possible to heal old wounds. If these experiences can be safely revealed, they can eventually be released.

I believe there is a hurt child (in varying degrees) within most of us, and as long as we ignore that child's voice there will be obstacles to the smooth functioning of the built-in healing system. None of this is said to judge or condemn anyone. I see it as a problem of our society as a whole. Infants and young children are more aware and more sensitive than we sometimes realize.

Although the problem exists worldwide, no one wants to talk about it or hear about it, and there are no easy solutions. By bringing up this painful subject I hope it will help more people to remember their own inner child with love and compassion.

With the perspective of maturity and experience, and maybe with the help of a trusted friend or a professional, consider replacing old patterns with healthier ones. If you want to work with your inner child, here are some steps you can take. Allow as much time as you need to work with each step.

HEALING YOUR INNER CHILD

The first step is to recognize that there were painful early experiences, and make a decision to look at them.

Try to re-experience the situation, knowing you are safe now.

As painful as it is, relate to the child you were, and how you must have felt at the time.

Allow yourself to feel the sadness. It's okay to grieve the loss of a happy childhood.

Recognize who is responsible, so you can stop blaming yourself.

Forgive—not condone—those responsible, to end your own suffering.

Most important, re-parent yourself in many ways, and treat yourself with kindness and gentleness.

Tell Your Story

"Sharing hidden secrets deepens you and makes you strong."
Unknown

People often wonder why God allows there to be so much suffering in the world. And someone quipped, "Because otherwise no one would talk to Him!" So if you need to unburden yourself of uncomfortable feelings that are holding you back, talking to God is a good place to start. Obviously, God is the comforter chosen by millions of people around the world.

In our modern society, many people go to therapists of various kinds to talk about their problems. Others say we should just leave the past behind. But from my experience, I believe that true healing requires facing the painful past deeply enough to be able to see it from a new perspective. Only then can you truly let it go. If you believe you were abused as a child, and would like to get professional help, be sure to find someone specifically trained in child abuse treatment. Such a person can provide a safe space for remembering thoughts and feelings that have been buried away. Many therapists do not have that special training.

Journaling is the practice of writing down your story, your thoughts, your fears, your dreams. It can be very therapeutic. It is the healing method of choice for many people who are not likely to seek outside help. Here are some suggestions:

TIPS FOR JOURNALING

Set a specific schedule for writing, such as fifteen minutes a day for four days in a row, or one day a week for a month, or whatever is right for you.

Don't plan to share your writing—that could inhibit your honest expression. Save it or destroy it, as you wish.

Explore your deepest thoughts and feelings, and why you feel the way you do. Write about your negative feelings such as sadness, shame, hurt, hate, anger, fear, guilt, or resentment. Don't judge yourself for having these negative feelings.

Write continuously. Don't worry about grammar, spelling, or making sense. If you run out of things to say just repeat what you have already written.

Support groups such as Alcoholics Anonymous (AA), or other twelve-step groups, are quite successful in helping people recover from addictions and other problems by providing a safe, non-judgmental place to share their stories and express their feelings.

Telling your story enables you to see it more objectively. Sharing long held secrets is good for your health, too, because it relieves you of the stress of keeping it locked inside. It frees the heart, making us more compassionate toward others. Think of the oyster and the pearl. It is the irritation of a grain of sand lodged inside the oyster's shell, that causes it to create the pearl, as protection from the injury. We too can create pearls—of wisdom—from our injuries.

Love Yourself

*"Use your mindfulness to hold your own inner pain
like a mother holds a baby."*

Thich Nhat Hanh

*D*id you ever notice that there are some things about you that just are? Always were, always will be. What you reject and what you enjoy. What interests you and what does not. No matter who loves you or who doesn't, there is something there that is always you. It is the essence of who you are. It is indescribable, but it directs your path. This is the real you. There is no effort involved in being who you are. It is there underneath the expectations of parents, teachers and society, waiting to be recognized.

On the way toward healing your emotions you can begin to remember who you really are, and to accept yourself as you are. Realize that every child deserves unconditional love and approval—including the child you once were. As a mature compassionate adult, you can be the one who sees the best in you and comforts you when you're down. After all, whose approval do you really want, or need? Who knows best what is true for you?

You must learn to love yourself—not because you think you are better than everyone else, but because you, like everyone else, needs and deserves to be loved—as you are, faults and all. Instead of being your own worst critic, you can be your own best supporter. Many of us walk around with a critical parent voice in our heads saying things like, "You're no good. You'll never amount to anything." If you have a voice like that in your head, you now have my permission to talk back to it. Don't believe it. Replace that outdated message with nurturing words instead, such as, "That was a really good try. You're getting it now." Be the parent who holds you, appreciates you, supports you in your trials and errors and empathizes when you fall. Consider that those who failed you may have had their own critical parent voices in their heads.

Know that whatever mistakes you may have made in the past, you were doing the best you could under the circumstances, and with the knowledge you had at the time. Remind yourself that now that you know better, you can do better. Realize that you are now, and always have been, worthy of love and respect. Re-building the sense of self-worth means unlearning the false belief that you aren't good enough. It means taking good care of yourself by expressing your needs and wants, and by setting boundaries. It also means looking for the positive qualities in yourself and in others. Getting involved with friends and support groups helps, as well as finding ways to express your creativity. Developing self-esteem is a necessary step toward health and happiness and success in life.

Remember that love is an action verb. It is about what we do and how we act toward other people—and it begins with loving ourself. Although we want to be good, kind people all the time, it's almost impossible when we're busy protecting ourselves from hurt, judging ourselves for every mistake, and feeling guilty and worthless. How can we be loving and kind to others when we feel sad, depressed and needy.

Acknowledge what you have been through and all you have experienced. Self-acceptance does not have to be earned. You deserve it—we all do. Those emotional gaps need to be filled, and as adults no one can do it for us. It is too late to expect it from parents and we can't expect it from partners or friends. Appreciating yourself as you are, allows you to improve and grow and flourish. It determines the quality of your life. It is the attitude of self-confidence and self-acceptance that attracts love and friendship, whereas self-judgment makes it difficult to connect at all. Let your posture and your attitude reflect your decision. Show the world who you really are. Love is your basic nature.

Don't Worry, Be Happy

"Happiness is not something ready made.
It comes from your own actions."

The Dalai Lama

When I was a teenager my father told me I should just stop worrying and be happy. He was reading *The Power of Positive Thinking,* by Norman Vincent Peale, one of the early books on the subject. I was disdainful, as teenagers can be, and I told him that there are serious things in life and I can't make believe I'm happy when I'm not! Later on, in the seventies, I heard the same message from one of the spiritual teachers in San Francisco. He said we should just "look, act and be happy"—even if we're not—and suggests that as a result the conditions in our life will improve by themselves. I finally conceded that even in the midst of problems, just putting on a happy face could change my entire outlook. Or, as some say, "Fake it 'til you make it!" The Dalai Lama reminds us that happiness comes from our own kind actions. His book *The Art of Happiness* is filled with more of his joyful wisdom.

Even while we are still dealing with the painful parts of our life, we could make a decision to be happy and to see things with a new attitude. We could begin at any time to start a new life of our own making. It only takes a switch of perspective, a new thought, and the realization that although pain exists, how we look at it determines how much we suffer. I have noticed that when I focus on complaining and feeling frustrated, I lose my strength and my wisdom. In order to be all I can be, I have to make a conscious decision to be happy. But I try not to make it another difficult task. I don't want to be miserable about not being happy. Then I have two problems! As Bobby McFerrin sings in his lively song, *Don't Worry, Be Happy:* "In every life we have some trouble, but when you worry you make it double, so don't worry, be happy."

Worry is a big deterrent to being happy. When we worry we are using our imagination (imagery) to create what we don't want just by focusing on it. And besides, worrying about something that might happen in the future makes us as unhappy now as if the feared situation had already taken place! Since the future doesn't exist, it may never happen at all. I have learned to watch what I imagine and what I say. Regretting the past and fearing the future can become a bad habit, and sometimes those negative thoughts consume me. But when I stay focused in the present, not only am I happier, but I am better able to think of solutions to prevent the situation I fear.

Worry about the future and resentment about the past are natural and understandable emotions. But it helps to remember that now is the only time there is, and let the rest go. Justifiable anger has its proper place, certainly outrageous things are happening in the world these days. But when we are angry, depressed and despairing we are contributing to the negativity that already exists. Instead, we do what we can to help and try not to add to the problems. We can take time to appreciate all the blessings in life. Without denying our feelings, we can choose to look at the bright side of events and help those around us to see the lighter side too.

Oh, what would we humans do without our sense of humor? Laughter is such a gift. Some years ago, a doctor in Bombay (Mumbai), India, realizing that people in his crowded city were suffering from too much stress, called people together just to laugh. Soon hundreds of people were gathering in a park in the center of town early in the morning. They didn't even bother telling jokes, they just started with "ha ha ha, ho ho ho, hee hee hee," and soon everyone joined in, laughing uncontrollably at the silliness of it all. Laughing, as we all know, is catching, and the people continued laughing for about an hour. The doctor noticed that the health of the people in Bombay improved as a result. This ongoing event, called The Laughing Clubs of Bombay, was reported in a major magazine and has been imitated in other places around the world. You can start your own laughing club, even a club of one! And don't forget—he who laughs at himself will never cease to be amused.

Norman Cousins, in *Anatomy of an Illness*, described how he healed himself of a medically incurable neurological disease by watching old funny movies with Charlie Chaplin or Buster Keaton (choose your favorite), and reading funny books. He did that for hours every day and literally laughed himself well!

I knew a jolly old-woman named Norma who attended a senior center where I taught one of my self-healing classes. She loved to tell jokes, sometimes off-color ones. One day she challenged me in a good-humored way: "I don't do any of the things you say we should do, but I'm healthy." My response was, "It's your wonderfully joyful attitude that keeps you so well, I'm sure. That's the most important thing." Ten years later, still attending the center, she told the class that whenever people ask for her secret to long life she tells them, "Good sex," and added, "That always gets 'em." She laughed out loud. We all did. Two months after that she died, just ten days before her one-hundredth birthday.

I don't mean to be glib, or to minimize the weight of anyone's painful emotions. I know what suffering feels like, and I know it can't be taken lightly. When a loved one dies, for instance, sadness and grief are not easily changed into laughter, nor should they be. Again, we don't want to repress our feelings, but to feel them fully. They say you have to grieve it before you can leave it. The goal is to eventually be able to focus on the happy memories, and then move on. Loneliness can be overwhelming until we can shift our attitude and begin to appreciate "aloneness" as a precious time to look within and to take care of ourselves. When we are ready we will go out and enjoy life again.

If it is true that the basic reality of life is harmony, then clearly it must be difficult or impossible to attune to that harmony while feeling anger, anxiety, or any other negative emotion. It would be easier when we are feeling kindness and compassion, would it not? In that state we would feel "in harmony," or "tuned in." We would return to the state of homeostasis where the body-mind system is in balance and working smoothly. Knowing that happiness releases healing chemicals in the brain that affect the whole body, we aim to make positive healthy choices.

Finally, don't forget to treat your senses while healing your emotions. Your senses determine what you feel—what you see, hear, taste, smell and touch. Even in the midst of suffering you can deliberately soothe your emotions. Keep active and interested and involved in things you enjoy. Listen to your favorite music—something lively to make you want to dance, something peaceful to help you relax, music that inspires you, or music that makes you smile. Walk barefoot on the sand or the grass, or get a foot massage. Take a long hot bath—with candlelight perhaps. Bake cookies—and eat them. Have a piece of chocolate—without feeling guilty. Clean the house with lively music playing. Wear a bright colored shirt. Sit in the sun for a while. Hug a friend. Smile—even for no reason. And easiest of all, don't forget to take a few nice…refreshing…slow…deep… in-breaths, with nice long out-breaths.

Treating your senses a little bit every day will slowly convince your mind that all is well. Your body will gear up for the long haul and will reward you with good health and long life.

Part Four

Spirit

Religion and Spirituality

"We are spiritual beings having a human experience."
Teilhard de Chardin

Whenever I remember to follow Bobby McFerrin's, and my father's, advice about not worrying and being happy, I become naturally more peaceful. The more I understand the effect my negative emotions have on me, and as I learn to be happy, the easier it is to flow into a spiritual state where I am more forgiving and more accepting.

Religion and spirituality are almost the same, but whereas religion refers to institutions that aim to teach their followers rules of behavior that lead to a connection to God, or divine truth, spirituality is the essence of religion. Spirituality is about finding inner peace, meaning and truth. Religion is an organized route for getting there. The goals of religion and spirituality are the same, although their methods and approach are quite different.

Although the spiritual (or religious) is the subtlest of the four aspects of who we are, it significantly affects them all—calming the emotions, quieting the mind and healing the body. I have noticed that when I give attention to the spiritual level through meditation, prayer, reading inspirational books, or taking a walk in nature, I tend to see the bigger picture and I become calmer and a little wiser.

My approach to spirituality is unconventional, a synthesis of many different teachings and practices, both ancient and modern, as well as insights from my personal experiences. In addition, I have been following recent discoveries in science that are shedding new light on the spiritual nature of reality. My goal in this chapter is not to promote or challenge any particular belief system, but simply to offer my personal insights, and to show how a spiritual perspective can affect physical health.

While I have never belonged to any type of organized religious or spiritual group, spirituality has been the undercurrent of my life. Knowing that the basic force, or intention, of the universe is love and goodness, changes my perspective on everything. I always look for a higher purpose. I see problems as opportunities to recognize where I have gone wrong, and I try to use them as lessons that help me do better. I aim for spiritual solutions such as patience, acceptance, trust, humor, and looking at the bright side. This approach to life may be defined as religious, or spiritual, or simply as a positive attitude.

Spirituality is a way of thinking about the meaning of life and who we are. Teilhard de Chardin, the Catholic theologian, said, "We are not human beings immersed in a spiritual experience. We are spiritual beings having a human experience." Are we really *spirit*, temporarily living in these human bodies? Or are we just physical bodies with brains trying to live a decent life? If you believe you are simply physical, the struggles of life might seem meaningless, and perhaps lead to feelings of despair. On the other hand, if you believe you are basically spirit, then you might only need to relax and rediscover the inner peace and harmony that is your true nature. You could trust that everything is as it should be, and you could stop struggling.

Surely these are troubled times. To relax makes us feel vulnerable. Our built-in emergency survival systems are working overtime leading to chronic stress, and we often feel tense and angry. We wonder where God is when we need Him/Her/It the most. Maybe He is right here, waiting for us to transcend the part of our nature that is based on defensiveness, competition, revenge, judgment and resentment, and live as the spiritual beings we really are, based on love. Kindness and compassion, tolerance and forgiveness, cooperation and respect are spiritual qualities. Where those qualities prevail, we may say that God exists.

Changing Attitudes

"Changing your attitude changes how you feel."

Unknown

There are two things that make up our experience—whatever is happening in our life at any moment, and our attitude toward that situation. It could be about certain people and how they treat us; the place we live and whether it's good enough or big enough; or a thing, and whether we want it, need it, hate it, or want more of it.

If you don't like a situation, but there is no way to change it—yet, the spiritual approach would be to choose an attitude of acceptance. That allows you to return to a state of peace and harmony and good will. Some people think "accepting" means being apathetic, or weak and resentful, but actually the opposite is true. Peacefully accepting things as they are comes from clear vision and inner strength. It brings a feeling of relief and calm. In that state of mind, although there are still wants and needs, they may be expressed as prayers, or affirmations, or as steps to action. Acceptance is a way of changing an attitude of hopelessness into one of faith in goodness. With faith we would imagine what we would like to happen, and see it as already done, while at the same time we would accept what we have with gratitude. With such faith and peaceful acceptance anything is possible.

The well-known Serenity Prayer of Alcoholics Anonymous says, "God grant me the serenity to accept the things I cannot change, the courage to change the things I can, and the wisdom to know the difference." I like to say it backwards: God grant me the wisdom to know what can be changed and what cannot, and if I think it can be changed, please grant me the courage to try to change it, and if I cannot, grant me the serenity to accept it as it is. Either way, serenity is the goal.

If you believe, as I have suggested, that we are here in this life to learn and grow from our experiences, you could say that things are actually perfect the way they are. From this point of view there are no accidents and no coincidences. All the problems and conflicts in life are opportunities for learning to look at things in a more positive way, to make the best of them. I don't believe that some power in the universe planned it all as lessons or punishments, but when those problems arise we just do our best and learn what we can from the experience. Ram Dass (formerly Richard Alpert), the well known New Age teacher, in *Grist for the Mill,* refers to the grit that farmers add to the mill to help grind the grain. Those rough spots help us grow. Like working out at the gym, we get stronger. If you look at it that way "it's all good" (a modern affirmation). With a strong focus, and a strong positive attitude, changes are possible.

A friend of mine dreamed that she was struggling to climb a rough and craggy mountain. Off in the distance she saw a nice smooth mountain and she wished her mountain were so smooth. Then she noticed that people were trying to climb that mountain, but since there was nothing to hold on to, they kept slipping down. She woke up appreciating her lot in life.

Attitude is a state of mind. It is your point of departure—the position you choose to take regarding people, things, or life in general. It is based on every experience you have had since childhood, and the values and beliefs you have developed over your lifetime. Attitudes seem to be very fixed—habitual and automatic—but actually, you always have the chance to reconsider, to see if it might make sense to look at things in a different way. In fact, a healthy attitude could be to question your current attitudes, to consider other possibilities and explore other choices. You can always go back.

In 1975, Jerry Jampolsky founded *The Center for Attitudinal Healing*, now known as *Attitudinal Healing International*, located in Sausalito, California. For many years this group has helped terminally ill children and young adults and their families all over the world to change their attitudes of bitterness, anger, fear and resentment, to acceptance, compassion and forgiveness. And since, as Dr. Jampolsky mentioned, unforgiving thoughts release toxins in the body that can harm the immune system and every organ, a change of attitude may allow good health to return.

Check the negative and positive attitudes listed here and see if you recognize any of them. Look them over every so often to see where you stand. This is not intended for self-judgment or self-criticism, but only for the purpose of awareness and self-healing.

NEGATIVE ATTITUDES

condescending	hostile
sarcastic	fearful
judgmental	resentful
superior	self-serving
defeatist	critical
pessimistic	hopeless

POSITIVE ATTITUDES

accepting	optimistic
appreciating	caring
compassionate	kind
grateful	loving
cheerful	selfless
responsible	respectful

Spiritual Healing

"Make believe you believe."

Agnes Sanford

When my daughter was seven she had a large wart on top of her big toe that had been there for over a year. One day when I was cleaning up the kitchen and she was out playing, I had the passing thought, "I'm sure that wart can be healed if I pray for it." I had been reading a book called *The Healing Light,* by a spiritual healer named Agnes Sanford. I planned to pray later, and I continued wiping the kitchen table. About fifteen minutes later my daughter came running into the house yelling, "Mommy, mommy, my wart is going away!" Sure enough, it was a little smaller, and within a week it was gone.

Some people might call that a coincidence, but I prefer to believe that my casual statement of faith—"I'm sure it can be healed" (even before I actually prayed)—was able to heal my daughter's toe almost instantly. If that is true, I have to think there must be some kind of power that exists beyond the normal. And if so I can tap into it when I need it. And it must be available to everyone.

Actually, all healing is spiritual healing. If we truly are spiritual beings temporarily in physical bodies, then who is in charge of keeping us healthy? Who is the "I" that decides to cooperate with the body's built-in healing system to help it function as intended? Who chooses to feed the body the right fuel to keep its engine running efficiently? Who notices our negative attitudes and chooses to change them to attitudes that will assure a more harmonious state of mind and body? Is it the body that cares and decides? What part of the body? Where is the caring part? Is it the thinking mind, filled with old conditioning and misunderstandings?

I suggest that only our own inner wisdom can be trusted with the delicate job of keeping our physical body in good repair. By understanding how precious a gift this body is, we realize we are blessed with the responsibility of caring for its needs. Practices such as counting our blessings, forgiving others, meditation and prayer, open us to that level of the universe that is harmonious. In that spiritual environment the healing forces can go to work.

We are more than a body and more than a mind. The body and the mind are connected to something universal—call it spirit, or consciousness. The body actually seems more like a vehicle, not unlike a spacesuit—or an earthsuit—designed for surviving on planet earth. I suggest that our own higher self, or spirit self, is the essence of us that is navigating this vehicle.

"Miracle" healings, ones that can't be explained by medical science, are often attributed to individual or group prayers, and other healing rituals or ceremonies. Bernie Siegel, M.D., in *Love, Medicine and Miracles*, talks about witnessing such healings with some of his patients. Dr. Andrew Weil's book *Spontaneous Healing,* also describes recoveries with no medical cause that resulted from mind-body-spirit "medicine," such as prayer and visualization and imagery. These unexplained healings are an indication that the physical body has the capacity to self-correct. When that happens, some people call it a miracle.

Agnes Sanford worked her healing magic during the First World War, when she visited injured soldiers in the hospital and prayed for them. When I heard her speak in Washington,

D.C., in 1960, she said she told the soldiers to trust that God would heal them, and to visualize themselves completely well, running and playing football. When one soldier said he didn't believe in God, she advised him to make believe he believed. She explained, in her charming way, that the act of believing—even if you have to fake it—is the magic switch that turns on the healing power that is always there, in the same way that electricity and water are there in our homes just waiting to be tapped. Many forms of spiritual healing exist, Western and Eastern as well as shamanic traditions. They all work with the powers of thought and energy and the belief in a higher force, or higher intelligence.

Bear in mind that disease has always been with us and it exists everywhere in nature. We should never blame ourselves if we get sick. The body has a mind of its own, responding to many different factors not always in our control. So even though the body listens to our thoughts, and reacts according to our wishes—even unconscious ones—getting sick is not your fault. Besides, feeling guilty is bad for your health.

Spiritual healing aims to counteract the fears that keep the doors and windows of the soul shut. It seeks to restore harmony through inspiration and trust. By taking a spiritual approach to life, you choose to allow the light of a new possibility to shine into the corners of the dark fortress. Let go of the protective tension, and allow relief to come. Breathe in, and breathe out, and allow real strength to arise in your body. Allow your built-in healing system to work.

As we have seen, healing the body is more than just fixing parts. Rachel Naomi Remen, M.D., professor at the University of California San Francisco School of Medicine, said, "We physicians need to reclaim the sacred nature of the work. Healing is not a matter of technique or mechanism; it is a work of spirit. True healing," she said, "is not just about the recovery of the body...more often it's about the recovery of the soul." As she pointed out, the soul wants to know that we love life and that we want to keep on living. The "will to live" sends the body a strong message, and it responds with increased healing activity.

Ruth St. Denis, the innovative dancer of the early 1900s in her recently reprinted book, *Wisdom Comes Dancing*, offered a similar perspective. "Too often, healing is just the mending of the broken instrument, a stringing of it up to pitch, but no new song is played upon it." While we need to fix whatever "fears and physical problems are causing any condition of illness," as she put it, for complete healing it is necessary to "restore the spiritual element of joy and the love of life."

Organized religions put it right in the hands of God. The sense of being comforted and supported, and a faith that all is well, opens us up to the healing forces. Studies of those who regularly attend religious services of any kind show that they have fewer illnesses, lower blood pressure, better immunity, less depression and recover faster from heart surgery, than those who do not. This is also true, I'm sure, for those who practice any form of spiritual faith.

Although there has been a long-time rift between science and religion, one based on material reality, the other based in the non-physical or supernatural level, they are beginning to come together in new and unexpected ways. As science delves deeper into the basic elements of life it is finding evidence that spiritual practices such as counting your blessings, forgiving yourself and others, meditation and prayer, have a powerful effect on healing the physical body. This kind of evidence is challenging the common belief of scientists that only physical methods, such as drugs and surgery, can heal the body.

Due to the nature of this new science the mind-body connection is not always provable with double-blind experimental conditions. Humans cannot be controlled like laboratory rats. There are too many variations among us with differing basic characteristics. In addition, the practice of mind-body methods involves skills not easily accomplished. This is a new concept to Westerners and a whole new mind-set is required. Certainly many people have seriously practiced these techniques, and healings have been accomplished, but there is no way to call these absolute proof. However, we can experiment on our own, and when it "works," we can be grateful. The more we practice we may become convinced, through the weight of evidence, that this is a valuable pursuit.

Approaching the connection between body, mind and spirit from the biological perspective, is the work of Bruce Lipton, Ph.D., cell biologist, who shows how the body's cells are affected by what we believe. His book *The Biology of Belief* is a fascinating account of the science behind holistic medicine.

This new joining of science and spirituality is uncovering things that are difficult to believe. However, the evidence is showing effects that cannot be explained, nor can they be denied. It is taking healing to a new level, the spiritual level, where metaphysical phenomena—meaning beyond, or outside of, physical reality—are being recognized as valid. Some forward thinking doctors are beginning to realize that in order to help their patients they must consider every treatment method available, even if it seems strange or impossible, as long as it can do no harm. Some are even praying with their patients. Larry Dossey, M.D., in *Reinventing Medicine,* suggested, half in jest, that doctors who didn't pray with their patients could be considered guilty of malpractice!

Dr. Dossey says that intuition is the first "screening." He tells us to pay attention to our gut feelings and to let our doctors know what we "get." By understanding that physical symptoms are the way the body tells us when something is malfunctioning, we know we must pay attention to the subtle hints we receive, and not ignore them or suppress them with pills. They are giving us a chance to correct or improve harmful habits.

Many people say they are unable to tune in to their gut feelings. It isn't easy, that's true. We have to learn to slow down and pay close attention before we can hear the body "talk." Taking some time each day to sit quietly, can help. You can become a scientist in your personal laboratory by experimenting with tuning in to minor ailments and following your hunches, and then observing the results of your actions. When you wake up in the morning, consciously direct healing thoughts and prayers to yourself, or to someone you know who is in need. Then watch for "miracles."

It is clear that there are many factors affecting human health that are non-physical, such as thoughts, feelings and faith. Although unexplainable recoveries are often called miracles, maybe they are really just examples of how things are supposed to be. In the opening pages of the modern spiritual book, A Course in Miracles, the word miracle is defined as "life working." Maybe all we have to do is remove obstacles, tune up the earthsuit and aim for goodness. It's a miracle—life works.

Daily Life, a Spiritual Exercise

"Forgiveness is giving up all hopes for a better past."
Gerald Jampolsky, M.D.

Daily life is a spiritual exercise in monasteries and temples. For us out here, daily life is often an exercise in frustration and futility. While most of us are rushing around multi-tasking and never looking back, monks seek the peace of God through being mindful while performing their daily chores. The question is, can we have both—our normal work and responsibilities and also mindful attention? Reuho Yamada, the young Japanese monk mentioned earlier, was raised in a monastery in Japan. While teaching a class in San Francisco, that I attended, he compared the whole world to a monastery, and even spoke of "the monastery of the car." Everything we encounter, he taught, can be used as an opportunity to practice the art of dealing with challenges in a peaceful way. The spiritual approach is to experience life with gratitude and appreciation, and in difficult times to ask, "What can I learn from this?" Or, "How did I get into this predicament, and how can I avoid it in the future?"

The myriad choices in life offer a wonderful school, with opportunities galore to practice holding positive attitudes in the midst of chaos. Of course there are terrible hardships in life and much suffering, but I trust that there is some kind of divine order that would reveal everything to be exactly as it should be—if only we could see the bigger picture. When life is thought of as a spiritual exercise we begin to notice all the blessings—sunrise and sunset, wild geese in formation, synchronicities, a child's smile—that often go unnoticed. And we can offer blessings to others with an unexpected phone call, a smile to a stranger, or "a random act of kindness." Rachel Naomi Remen's book *My Grandfather's Blessings,* recounts many heartwarming stories from her patients, and from her own personal life, that are filled with blessings and inspiration.

When, inevitably, negative thoughts about people or events appear, we can catch them and stop them in their tracks and send forth a little silent "bless it," or "bless them." In that way angry responses to other people can be checked, especially those habitual reactions to family members, or to other drivers on the road, or to certain people we see on television. Have you noticed how much energy is wasted in getting upset at people?

Think of all the old grudges we carry around. Can they be forgiven? To forgive a wrong action is not to accept or justify what was done, or the person who did it. The purpose of forgiveness is to let the painful experience go from your mind, no matter how bad, so you can stop suffering. In a way, forgiveness is a selfish act. We do it so we can feel better, not to change the other person. Of course, it isn't always easy to do. As one student of Buddhism said, "Forgiveness is the price you have to pay for peace of mind." It is a decision you make that has the power to change your life.

Leo Buscaglia, author of *Living, Loving and Learning,* was a joyful and loving man often seen on television before his death a few years ago. He told a story about a woman who had been badly beaten and mugged in her car while stopped at a traffic light. He went to visit her in the hospital in hopes of cheering her up and he found her bandaged from head to toe but with a bright smile on her face. He asked her, "How can you be so happy after what that man did to you?" Her reply was, "I gave him enough of my life and I'm not going to give him any more!"

In his wonderful little book *Forgiveness, the Greatest Healer of All,* Dr. Jampolsky points out that what happened in the past will never change no matter how much anger and resentment we hold, and that the only one hurt by these feelings is ourself. To forgive involves acknowledging what happened and recognizing how it feels. Only then can we truly let it go. We have to give up hopes for a better past, and move on with our lives.

Imagine how we could change the world (at least our own little worlds) by practicing forgiveness on a daily basis toward any rude remark, unkind attitude, or selfish behavior we run into. If love is, indeed, the natural state for human beings, then love must be the answer to "unlove." When I encounter people being selfish or angry I have to conclude that they must not have any love to give—at least at the moment. When I see it that way I feel motivated to be forgiving, rather than judgmental. Even more important than forgiving others, is to forgive myself for my many mistakes and slip-ups. When I allow myself some slack, it is easier to let other people off the hook when they make mistakes. It is just about remembering that we are all doing the best we can.

As I have pointed out before, love is something you do. It is not something you expect or wait for. It all starts with you! Love is our true nature. Be loving, kind and generous. Giving is the same as receiving because it feels so good to give. You don't have to give money or things—give of yourself, volunteer your time, be helpful where help is needed and wanted. Assuming, as they say, we are all connected, then inevitably, when we lift each other up we all benefit.

Daily life becomes a spiritual exercise when we express gratitude for the blessings in our lives, and when we learn to see everything as a blessing—although sometimes in disguise. We live a spiritual life by behaving ethically and decently, considering the feelings of others and being kind, and by aiming to do no harm to people, animals, or the environment. We nurture a spiritual life when we remember to connect with nature in some way each day, even if it is just to water a houseplant or look at the sky. While we go about our ordinary chores such as shopping, cleaning, putting out the garbage and even paying bills, daily life offers endless opportunities to act with mindfulness and acceptance of "what is."

Knowing how to live a spiritual life is an opportunity to heal these precious physical bodies of ours by honoring them with good loving care. It blossoms naturally out of an inner belief in the perfection of nature and the innate goodness of life. It comes from trusting that we are self-healing beings designed for survival, with every part of us working together for our good. Understanding this leads to good health from the inside out, eliminating the root causes of ill health so as to prevent the outer manifestations.

A spiritual life also includes some time for sitting quietly in meditation, contemplation, or prayer. Aside from the calming effects meditation has on the mind, it has been demonstrated to have a positive effect on the body as well. Deepak Chopra, M.D., endocrinologist and author of many books on health and spirituality, says, "By allowing us to enter a state of restful alertness in our mind, meditation literally transforms our body's chemistry." Learning to meditate on a regular basis is an important key to health and well being.

Although it is a basic component of all religions, meditation can be practiced by people who have no religious affiliation or spiritual beliefs. It can be thought of as a practical tool for improving your health, or as a personal quest to find the peacefulness in your own quiet mind. However, a trust in goodness, and a focus on some form of higher power, will deepen the experience. As Agnes Sanford said, if you don't believe in a higher power, "make believe you believe." All methods of meditation are good. Choose your own favorite one. The following meditation was adapted from the traditional Indian practice, Transcendental Meditation (TM), by Herbert Benson, Harvard psychology professor and author of *The Relaxation Response*. It is basically the same as the traditional Christian contemplative meditation called Centering Prayer. I have put it in my own words, and call it Simple Meditation.

SIMPLE MEDITATION

Set aside a period of time when you won't be interrupted, five minutes to start. After a while you might want to increase it to twenty minutes.

Get comfortable, sitting in a chair, or lying in bed.

Breathe slowly and evenly, close your eyes (or not), and relax your body as much as possible.

Choose a word or sound or phrase that has a peaceful meaning for you, such as: peace, I am at peace, relax, all is well. Repeat it on each exhalation. When you notice your mind wandering simply bring it back, and continue repeating the word or phrase.

When the time is up sit quietly for a few minutes, then slowly open your eyes, look around, and return to your day.

Each time you sit with the intention of doing nothing for a set period of time, even if you keep getting distracted, you are contributing to your body's healing and your peace of mind. Eventually you will learn to be still. You are training your mind, and that takes time. Have you ever tried to train a puppy to sit? You tell it to sit, and soon it gets up and wanders off. You gently pick it up and bring it back and tell it again to sit. Although you may have to do that a hundred times, the puppy finally learns. Your mind is the same. Simply bring it back, gently and lovingly, as soon as you catch it wandering off. You can say, silently or out loud, "Oh well," and tell it once more to be still. Or maybe you have monkey mind, a term used to compare our easily distracted minds to the way monkeys jump from tree to tree all day long. Whether you are like a puppy or like a monkey, you are not alone. It seems to be the nature of our minds to wander off and to jump from one thought to another. Don't try to force it. Just continue to relax, and allow your mind to settle down.

Not all meditations are practiced while sitting. Walking, when focusing on each step slowly and intentionally, is enjoyable and easy. T'ai Chi Chih is a meditation in motion, practiced slowly and with full awareness of each movement. Gardening and knitting can also be meditative, because attention is focused on one thing. Practicing some form of meditation for a little while every day teaches us to be more aware. We learn to be in the present moment, to just be. As Jon Kabat-Zinn asks, "Do you want to be a human being, or a human doing?"

Inner Peace and World Peace

*"The transformation of the world is brought about by
the transformation of one's self."*

J. Krishnamurti

Inner peace is surely a goal to be desired, but new challenges appear every day conspiring to disturb me. Knowing what I do about the importance of inner peace in preserving my health and increasing my longevity, I set myself the goal of peace, and I aim in that direction. Still, the state of the world can get me pretty anxious at times. That's when I try to remember that I can do more good by being cheerful than by being grumpy, no matter what happens, and I feel better besides. Staying peaceful requires constant awareness and practice.

But can you, should you, be peaceful at all costs? Where are the limits? Can you expect to remain peaceful even under the most trying of circumstances? Should you, can you, remain peaceful in the face of brutality or injustice? Would you want to achieve peace at someone else's expense? Does it make sense to fight for peace—or isn't that an oxymoron? Is it worth killing even one person for peace? Whose peace? Who benefits? These are questions that deserve to be examined by each of us. There are no black and white answers, and no one else can answer for you.

Aiming for peace is a gift you give yourself. Like forgiveness, it is not always easy but it has great rewards. Even in the middle of a busy active life you can take a few minutes every so often to stop and breathe and enjoy the moment. If peace is your goal, it helps to learn new ways to deal with the ordinary daily conflicts that lead to stress and tension in the home and workplace. For example, getting organized helps things go more smoothly, eliminating frustration. Solving problems clears the mind.

Conflict over ideas and beliefs starts wars, the big wars as well as little one-on-one wars. Interpersonal conflicts cause much of our pain and stress, with each party needing to be right. As Jerry Jampolsky asks, "Which is more important to you, to be right—or to be peaceful?" Can you understand the other person's point of view? Have you really heard that person's point of view? Has she or he heard yours?

As a Community Mediator, I learned the following simple rules of conflict resolution: each party involved gets a chance to describe his or her complaint without interruption, and then the other party repeats back what was said. When both sides are sure they have been heard, they brainstorm to find a solution, continuing until both are satisfied. That's it! Having an impartial moderator can help a lot, of course, but the most important requirement is that both parties agree to the process beforehand, and are willing to follow the simple but powerful rules.

If only nations and cultures could agree to follow the rules of conflict resolution, to listen to each other with an aim for understanding. If only they could forgive each other for age-old conflicts instigated by power-hungry leaders, and resolve their differences. Can we consider the radical concept that a point of view different from ours may have merit, and respect those who hold that opposing view? Can we accept the notion that everyone is right from his or her point of view? By recognizing the experiences that have led to our own viewpoints, can we also acknowledge the experiences of those we disagree with, and understand how they arrived at the beliefs they hold? Peace comes from allowing other people—friends and relatives as well as those from other cultures and religions—to differ with us. Can peace be forced on someone?

Thich Nhat Hanh, Buddhist monk, was nominated by Martin Luther King, Jr. for the Nobel Peace Prize for his efforts during the Vietnam War. He has dedicated his life to fostering peace in the world. His teachings are simple and universal: "Our appointment with life is now, the present moment. If peace and joy are not now, when?" The present moment, he tells us, is the only time that we are really in touch with life. The past is gone and the future doesn't exist. It is up to us to be peaceful now. In his little book *Peace Is Every Step,* Thich Nhat Hanh reminds us in many ways that peace and happiness are available in every moment. He teaches with charming images and simple meditations:

> **Breathing in, I calm myself.**
> **Breathing out, I smile.**
> **Breathing in, I dwell in the present moment.**
> **Breathing out, I feel it is a wonderful moment.**

Or, even easier: **Calming...Smiling...Present moment... Wonderful moment**. I practice this meditation, or some version of it, while breathing in and out slowly to calm my mind, to loosen all the tense muscles in my body, and to remember to smile. You can make up your own version of this meditation.

As a part of the world we each have a role to play in world peace. In these times of war and violence, economic problems and environmental disasters, smiling and calming our minds is an important contribution, and the least we can do. We can offer comfort to those around us with our patience and gentleness, our decency and goodness and our smiles. We can be an example to others by appreciating, and cooperating, and by recognizing what is real and important. We can see all the crises in the world as blessings in disguise—waking us up to think for ourselves and learn compassion. It is an opportunity for transformation.

If we are not peaceful in ourselves and in our relationships, then we are part of the problem. We can't blame anyone else, because it is up to us. As Krishnamurti said, first we must transform ourselves, then the world will transform. Gandhi said the same thing in his own way: "You must be the change you wish to see in the world." As we learn to change ourselves we become teachers and helpers to others, passing on the lessons we have learned.

Every little change we make sends out waves, like the ripples from a pebble thrown into a pond, that affects others. As we forgive those who have harmed us in the past, and those with whom we disagree, we can release our violent thoughts and recover the sacred part of us. Release the past—let it go. If it was unhappy it was just a mistake anyway. As we become more peaceful we come back to our essence, which is love. And since everything in the universe is interconnected, when each one of us is peaceful the planet is healed.

Healers from many cultures believe that the primary cause of illness is spiritual, not physical. A lack of meaning or purpose, and uneasiness about the world in general, keep us spiritually disconnected. Feelings of helplessness and despair can make us sick. Let us acknowledge that our civilization is in trouble, and all the strife we hear about through the media is very disturbing. But times like these are an opportunity to reevaluate where we have gone wrong, and perhaps to change our ways.

There is much to be sad about and much to be angry about.

Let us do what we can to change things for the better, and know that the one thing we can always change for the better is our own attitude. When we do we become healthier and happier, and by example, we become part of the solution instead of part of the problem. Trust that everything is working for the good of all, even if it isn't evident now. Trust is the spiritual fertilizer that feeds new understanding and new growth. The key to spiritual healing is to give thanks for the blessing of being alive.

Part Five

Pain, Aging, Dying

Give Love to Your Pain

"All pain, regardless of the cause, is made worse by tension."
Unknown

Pain plays a very important role in protecting the body. If there were no pain reflex we might touch a hot burner and not pull our hand away, walk on a broken leg, or ignore the warning signs of a heart attack. As part of the design for survival, pain calls attention to something out of order. It is a necessary part of the plan. But that's not how we feel about it when it is occurring. We want to block it from our minds however possible. Darn this sore knee, we think, now I can't play ball, or dance, or walk! Unconsciously, we clench the muscles around the pain to try to avoid feeling it, or walk on a sore foot, making it worse. We take pain pills, thinking if we don't feel it, it isn't there. While this might work temporarily, and can be valuable in that regard, we need to go deeper. Instead of trying to block the pain, we need to give it our full attention so it knows it has been heard.

You could think of pain as a call for help, like a baby crying for his mother's attention. As the philosopher Samuel Johnson said, "Pain concentrates the mind wonderfully." It blots out all other considerations until it gets the attention it requires. If you reject it, it calls louder. When you give it loving attention the muscles soften and the pain lessens. Of course, you want to love the part of the body that feels the pain—not the pain itself! The knee, the shoulder, the back, or whatever, are a part of you that is hurting. You soothe and comfort it, and talk to it sweetly as you would to a hurt child: "There there, you'll be all right." As we have seen, the body responds to our thoughts.

When pain is severe, and when it is constant, it may be almost impossible to focus on these suggestions. But I believe it is especially important to try the mind-body techniques offered here before bombarding the body with powerful chemicals. However, because the stress and strain on the whole system that results from chronic pain can be very debilitating, and can lead to other problems, some form of pain medication may be necessary, and a blessing.

Some pain clinics around the country are using the Buddhist technique of "mindfulness meditation," a program started by Jon Kabat-Zinn at the University of Massachusetts. People who suffer from chronic pain are encouraged to deal with it directly, rather than blocking awareness of it with medications. The patients learn to observe the pain without anger or resentment, and to have compassion for their own suffering. They learn to "talk to the pain," and ask it what it needs. Often, surprising answers come to mind. Instead of being overwhelmed victims, they become active participants in the healing process.

Becoming calmer removes some of the tension from the problem area. All pain is made worse by tension, because the tense muscles put pressure on the surrounding nerves, which aggravates the initial problem. In addition, tension blocks the flow of blood and energy to the painful area, interfering with natural healing. It takes trust to let go of the protective muscle tension. It seems that to do so would make the pain worse, but actually, it helps.

For many years, I have practiced resisting the instinct to clutch the injured area, grimace and yell Ow! Ow! Ow! after spraining my ankle, stubbing my toe, or burning my hand on the hot oven. My natural tendency is to overreact, but I have learned to counteract that impulse by getting very calm. I take a deep breath and release it fully. Calmly but quickly I put ice (or a bag of frozen peas) on the burn, or hold the ankle or toe, reassuring it until it feels better. Sometimes I help my healing system along with a "mental placebo." I tell my body I have given it an aspirin, or antibiotics, even when I haven't! Imagery, as we discussed earlier, can often cause the same effects in the body chemistry as the real thing.

Again, the question is, who is the healer? Who is suffering and who is helping? The body needs help, and the mind comes to the rescue. It calls on all the body's healing forces: Attention! Awareness needed in the lower back! Discomfort in the lower back! Attention! And the emotional part of us, the one that suffers and is afraid, is comforted by the attention and the care. The body relaxes so the powerful internal healing forces can systematically go about their business repairing and adjusting what is out of balance. Then the spirit within us sends love and life force energy to bring the body back to harmony. The healer is the spirit in you.

In short, learn to see each symptom as a call for love and attention, because resistance only makes it worse. Rather than being at war with yourself, direct compassionate thoughts to the painful body that has endured so much conflict, and soothe your hurting self. The following meditation practice may help.

BRING COMPASSION TO PAIN

Gently close your eyes and notice your breathing.

Center your attention on the pain; notice the feelings.

Accept what you find without resistance.

Let your breath flow through the painful area.

Send thoughts of compassion to the pain.

Accept the part of your body that is having pain now.

Pay attention to the circumstances creating the pain.

Guide yourself to be peaceful and free from fear.

Rest your attention on the area of discomfort.

When you are ready, end the meditation by returning to your breath for a short while.

Enjoying Life Longer

"People don't grow old. When they stop growing they become old."
Aldous Huxley

I once worked on a publication in Mendocino, California, called *Country Women Magazine*. The topic of one issue was "Older Women." At forty, I felt qualified to write about getting old. But when twenty-nine year old women wrote about their horror of turning thirty, I suddenly realized that aging is a relative concept. In fact, aging begins at birth. I recalled how old I felt when I turned six. Where is the dividing line between young and old? What, in fact, is middle age?

Robert Butler, M.D., founding director of the National Institute on Aging, said "We haven't found any biological reason not to live to 110." Other experts on aging have suggested that barring unforeseen events such as accidents or disease, the normal lifespan for humans is at least 120 years. In that case, sixty would be middle age—with another sixty to go!

Like everything else, our bodies work best when they are new. We tend not to notice the subtle damage that is gradually taking place, and it goes unnoticed for years. When we're young we can't imagine aging or dying so we ignore the little warning signals. Habitually, we take in the wrong kind of fuel, burn the candle at both ends, and wear ourselves out. It is easy to forget that every experience we have ever had has formed the body in which we now live. "Our biography becomes our biology," said author Carolyn Myss. Every day we unconsciously make choices between behaviors that allow our bodies' systems to operate efficiently and with ease, and behaviors that lead to premature aging.

Albert Schweitzer, M.D., the great humanitarian doctor, and Pablo Casals, the world famous cellist, are models of accomplished men who, into their later years, had a sense of purpose and a strong will to live. Each one played Bach on the piano every day. It was their medicine. Pablo Casals had very severe crippling arthritis that totally disappeared when he played the piano. Dr. Schweitzer said disease "found little hospitality" inside his body. "I have no intention of dying," he said, "so long as I can do things, and if I do things there is no need to die. So I will live a long, long time." Norman Cousins related these stories in his book, *Anatomy of an Illness*. Aldous Huxley, author of *Brave New World*, and other provocative books, was another man with a strong will to live. He was in his later years when he suggested that people grow old when they stop growing.

These stories and quotations that I have collected through the years have inspired me to change my attitude, and the words I use, in talking about getting older. It would be easy to blame all my problems on aging, thus reinforcing the expectation of inevitable decline. Or I could joke about the foibles of aging, but that too reinforces the expectation, and I'm trying not to fall into these habits. I know that how I think and talk affects my body. Mainly I choose to think like my student, Andy, in his seventies. I opened my class one day with the question, "What does aging mean to you?" I expected to begin a discussion. But Andy's hand shot up in the back of the room and he said, "Nothing!"

Ellen Langer, a professor in the psychology department of Harvard University, carried out an experiment in 1979 that demonstrated the power of the mind-body connection with respect to aging. She took a group of 100 men from a nursing home, to a week-long retreat. They were all seventy to eighty years old. They went to a place designed to look and feel like the year 1959, with magazines and equipment from that year. The men were told to bring family photos from 1959, none more recent. Elvis Presley music was playing on the record player. At the end of only one week all the men showed improvement of their eyesight, hearing and blood pressure, and even their joints had become more flexible. In her book, *Counter Clockwise*, Dr. Langer describes the study, and the conclusions drawn from it.

We all have three different ages at any one time, chronological or actual numeric age, biological or physical condition age, and psychological age, or how old we feel. The men in the study reduced their biological age by psychologically feeling younger! The controlled environment they were in reinforced feeling young. In our environment, television reinforces the fear of aging by trying to sell us products designed to avoid getting old. It is difficult to counteract that negative influence. Aging has been called a self-fulfilling prophecy. The more you expect it, fear it and focus on it, the more you begin to feel old, act old, and allow your body to slowly give up its will to live. What is your real age? How young do you feel?

Aiming to stay healthy and enjoy life longer is not about denying the aging process. It is about appreciating each and every stage for what it is. We are seeing many people these days doing just that. Without denying they are getting chronologically older, they keep an open mind, stay involved, have friends of all ages and keep learning. Let us cultivate beauty, and health in general, out of self-love and self-acceptance rather than to avoid signs of aging. Beauty shines from within. Regret, and the envy of youth, undermine our beauty.

At the same time, when disabilities come upon us that slow us down, we can accept that fact peacefully and even learn from it. Ram Dass (formerly Richard Alpert), the well-known author of *Be Here Now*, youth icon and popular spiritual teacher, was writing a book about aging. He was in his mid-sixties, healthy and active, playing golf and enjoying life. Not sure how to finish his book, he decided to "research" the question by imagining being a very old man with real physical challenges. When the phone rang in the middle of his fantasy he got up to answer it, but his leg gave way under him and he fell to the floor. He picked up the phone but was unable to form the words to respond. He had had a stroke—a massive cerebral hemorrhage so severe that he almost died. A few years, and a lot of physical therapy later, Ram Dass, although still in a wheelchair, recovered enough to finish his book. The stroke had provided him with the information and experience he needed. With his characteristic wisdom and good humor Ram Dass describes what he learned in *Still Here: Embracing Aging, Changing and Dying.*

"Age works to our advantage spiritually," he wrote, "it spiritualizes us naturally, giving us time to go deeper into faith and connect with our heart and soul. Some experience old age as the greatest stage in the life process." Life can be seen as having three stages, he explains, the first for growing up and learning, the second for service to family and the community, and the last for oneself. It is a chance to discover our true self, to reevaluate our attitudes and beliefs. Each person is unique, of course. We each have the opportunity to choose our path according to our own needs and abilities and inclinations, and to see every day as part of our path. This is the time for letting go of expectations and feeling free to just be.

I want to end this chapter on aging with another provocative quote from Ram Dass: "You spent the first half of your life becoming somebody. Now you can work on becoming nobody, which is really somebody. For when you become nobody there is no tension, no pretense, no one trying to be anyone or anything. The natural state of the mind shines through unobstructed, and the natural state of the mind is pure love."

Everyone Here Dies

"The doctor dies as well as the patient. The king dies as well as the servant. This is a place where everyone dies."

Ravi Shankar

Since nobody can tell us exactly what dying is about, there is naturally a lot of speculation. I've heard it said that "life is a temporary assignment." We all know we will die, but we ask ourselves, have we really lived? It changes the perspective when we think about the meaning of life and acknowledge the inevitability of death. As the world famous Indian musician, Ravi Shankar, bluntly pointed out, everyone here dies.

When it comes down to it most of us are scared, and we need to talk about it. The late Elisabeth Kubler-Ross, M.D., author of *On Death and Dying*, said, "In our unconscious mind we can't imagine the end of life. We are designed by nature to survive. The bodymind works continuously to protect itself and to prolong life, so it is naturally afraid of death." In her classic book, she describes the five stages that many people go through when they are dying: denial (this can't be true), anger (why me!), bargaining (God, if you let me live I promise to be good), depression (poor me—what's the use), and finally, acceptance. Most people need to work through each of these stages until they come to some level of acceptance. Friends and loved ones need to, as well. Knowing that life is a temporary assignment, we all need to be ready for "graduation."

Dr. Kubler-Ross explained that since most of us are conditioned to believe we are nothing more than bodies and minds, we naturally fear old age and death, because it would mean we cease to exist. But in many cultures people accept death as a natural part of life, and they are not afraid of it. In India people live as souls, and death is expected and prepared for. For them, death is like coming to the end of a book they are reading.

When I was in Bali, Indonesia, I attended a funeral, which in that culture is viewed as a celebratory event. A huge brightly colored structure is built in the shape of a sacred cow. The body of the deceased is placed inside the structure and carried through the streets in a colorful and noisy procession, with Balinese drums and musical instruments playing. The whole community, including tourists, joins in the spectacular event. When it reaches its destination the whole cow with the body in it is set on fire, accompanied by the hauntingly beautiful Balinese "gamelan" music sending the soul on its way.

If, as I have suggested, the body is the vehicle that houses the spirit—the essence of who we are—then to die may be nothing more than the stepping out of the vehicle while our "self" moves on. Or, we could think of the body as a garment, or our "birthday suit," that serves us well, eventually becomes worn out with use, and is finally ready to be discarded. Believing that we are more than a body may help to remove the fear of death.

None of us know what to expect after death, yet some spiritual teachers have described it as a birth into another realm. They say there will be beings (midwives?) waiting to receive us and welcome us. All we have to go on are the descriptions of people who have come back to life shortly after being pronounced clinically dead. They all describe the "near death experience" as beautiful, and filled with love. They lose their fear of death.

While many scientifically minded people are skeptical, and explain the phenomenon as merely a chemical change that happens in the brain when it is deprived of oxygen, all the reports from those who have had near-death experiences seem to indicate that it feels like something holy.

For the skeptics, I offer this tale of twins in the womb talking to each other. The girl twin says, "I believe that there is a place where there is light, and space to move around, and that someday we will go there. And I also believe that there is something called a Mother." The boy twin says, "That's ridiculous! You're crazy! This dark, crowded space is all there is, get used to it, and you have no proof that a Mother exists!"

What is this thing called dying that invades the thoughts and fears of so many people? For me, if there is even the possibility of a place with more light, more space, and more love, I'll hold to that hope. It encourages me to prepare myself by living well, to be ready to graduate from this open-ended school we live in when that time comes.

I'm sure the body will object, kicking and screaming. It was designed for survival on this earth. It was built to last. But like an astronaut who removes the space suit that was designed for survival in space when returning home, we too must eventually shed our suit.

> *"When I arrived in this world, I was crying, and*
> *everyone else was laughing, and when I left this world,*
> *I was laughing and everyone else was crying!"*
>
> Kabir, 15th Century Persian poet

Part Six

Summary

Letting Go: the Key

As we have seen, mind-body medicine refers to the healing effects that come from understanding and working with the interaction between the mind and the body. Since every negative event, large or small, shuts down or aggravates some part of the healing system, we want to try to clear the body of obstructions to allow the system to work effectively. The goal of mind-body medicine is to prevent potentially harmful effects on the body and increase the beneficial ones.

It appears that on every level letting go is the key to self-healing. Once we learn to become aware of where we are holding on, we will begin to recognize when to let go. And when we understand that we are more than a body, more than a mind, and more than our feelings, we can let go of attachment to these. When we do our spirit, the essence of us, remains.

Physically, we can release the "armoring" created by tense muscles and joints. The function of muscles is to contract when needed for movement and balance. When they are not needed we can let them go. Are you frowning? Holding your breath? Tensing your shoulders? Is there a need to?

Mentally, we can become aware of habits of thinking that do us no good, such as worrying, complaining, regretting, bearing grudges and other forms of negative thinking, and let them go. We can stop judging other people, and also stop judging ourselves. We can let go of thoughts about the past and the future, and just be here now.

Emotionally, we may be filled with grief and sadness, or fear based on the past even when the danger is long gone. Some experiences need time to heal, but eventually we can let go of the past and move on. Otherwise, old hurts and resentments may make us continue to feel victimized, or angry, or locked in depression. Examine any of your habitual reactions that are no longer appropriate, and try to let them go.

On the Spiritual level, fear and doubt may interfere with our ability to feel peaceful and loving. We are afraid that this is not a safe universe, and with that comes the fear of death. When we feel cut off, can we make a decision to trust in goodness and see what happens? Can we learn to let go of fear and doubt and focus on love instead so we can find happiness now?

With any kind of pain, minor or very serious, whether physical or emotional, releasing physical tension and relaxing as much as possible, will help. While our instinct is to hold on tighter to protect, we have to resist that urge, let go instead, and allow the inner healer to work.

As we get older, we can let go of conditioned images and concepts about aging and keep living to the fullest extent we can, as long as we can.

As the end of life approaches, hopefully we will be able to peacefully let go of attachment to the body.

Letting go is an ongoing practice. The protective function of every aspect of the bodymind system is so ingrained, and so fundamental, that our resistance to letting go is very strong and instinctive. But maybe the challenge of these changing times, when we are at a loss for answers, is to let go and let God.

BOOKS AND REFERENCES

Benson, Herbert. *The Relaxation Response*

Borysenko, Joan. *Minding the Body, Mending the Mind*

Bradshaw, John. *Healing the Shame that Binds You*

Buscaglia, Leo. *Living, Loving and Learning*

Carson, Rachel. *Silent Spring*

Chopra, Deepak. *Quantum Healing; Ageless Body, Timeless Mind*

Coué, Emil. *Self-Mastery through Conscious Auto-Suggestion*

Cousins, Norman. *Anatomy of an Illness*

Dass, Ram. *Grist for the Mill; Still Here*

Davis, Adelle. *Eat Right for Your Health*

de Chardin, Teilhard. *The Phenomenon of Man*

Dienstfrey, Harris. *Where the Mind Meets the Body*

Dossey, Barbara, Jeanne Achterberg, Leslie Kolkmeier. *Rituals of Healing*

Dossey, Larry. *Reinventing Medicine; The Power of Premonitions*

Feldenkrais, Moshe. *Awareness through Movement*

Gach, Michael Reed. *Acupressure's Potent Points*

Gil, Eliana. *Outgrowing the Pain: A Book for and about Adults Abused as Children*

Goleman, Daniel. *Mind-Body Medicine* (Consumer Reports)

Hay, Louise. *Heal Your Body; You Can Heal Your Life*

Holt, John. *How Children Learn; How Children Fail*

Jampolsky, Gerald. *Love Is Letting Go of Fear; Forgiveness: The Greatest Healer of All; Shortcuts to God*

Kabat-Zinn, Jon. *Wherever You Go, There You Are*

Krishnamurti, J. *Commentaries On Living; Think on These Things; Education and the Significance of Life*

Langer, Ellen. *Counter Clockwise*

Liedloff, Jean. *The Continuum Concept*

Lipton, Bruce. *The Biology of Belief; Spontaneous Evolution*

Lowen, Alexander. *Betrayal of the Body; Bioenergetics*

Miller, Alice. *Thou Shalt Not Be Aware; Banished Knowledge*

Nhat Hanh, Thich. *Peace Is Every Step; The Art of Power*
Northrup, Christiane. *Women's Bodies, Women's Wisdom*
Pearce, Joseph Chilton. *Magical Child Matures; The Biology of Transcendence*
Pert, Candace. *Molecules of Emotion; Your Body is Your Subconscious Mind*
Pollan, Michael. *The Omnivore's Dilemma*
Pollack, William. *Real Boys*
Price, Weston A. *Nutritional and Physical Degeneration*
Remen, Rachel Naomi. *My Grandfather's Blessings*
Rossman, Martin. *Healing Yourself with Mental Imagery*
Sanford, Agnes. *The Healing Light*
Sapolsky, Robert. *Why Zebras Don't Get Ulcers*
Selye, Hans. *The Stress of Life; Stress without Distress*
Siegel, Bernie. *Love, Medicine and Miracles*
Sobel, David. *Healthy Mind, Healthy Body Handbook;*
  with Robert Ornstein. *Healthy Pleasures*
St. Denis, Ruth. *Wisdom Comes Dancing*
Suzuki, Shunryu. *Zen Mind, Beginner's Mind*
Weil, Andrew. *Natural Health, Natural Medicine; Why Our Health Matters*

ORGANIZATIONS

Attitudinal Healing International., Sausalito, Ca. (www.AHInternational.org)

Foundation for Inner Peace, *A Course in Miracles*

La Leche League. *Womanly Art of Breastfeeding* (www.lalecheleague.org)

T'ai Chi Chih™, Joy Thru Movement (www.taichichih.org)

IN APPRECIATION

For his professional technical support, editing help, design and re-design of the layout and the cover, and for his endless patience beyond human endurance, I could never thank my husband Ted enough.

Without Terry Bloom, I would never have become a college instructor. For her ongoing support, advice and friendship I am forever grateful.

Much appreciation has to go to the hundreds of my adult students who attended my classes and encouraged me to put my teachings into a book.

I also thank my first editor, Caroline Charlesworth, for her skillful corrections. Although the manuscript has gone through many revisions since her early edits, I learned a lot from her and have tried to keep her main suggestions intact.

Mary Dale Scheller, who taught this subject before I did, was kind enough to read an early version, and to suggest some major revisions that forced me to improve my book.

And for all the writers and teachers and healers and leaders whose wisdom I have gathered and followed over the years, I am enormously indebted. I would not be the same person without their knowledge and insight. They shaped my life, and I feel privileged to pass their teachings on to my students and my readers.

ABOUT THE AUTHOR

Diane See is a writer, dancer, healer, educator, counselor, group leader and speaker. Her life studies in healthy human development from infancy to aging, and many years of dance training, went into the writing of this book.

Diane is a certified college instructor and an accredited T'ai Chi Chih™ instructor. She taught Mind-Body Health and T'ai Chi Chih at City College San Francisco for thirteen years. She is also accredited in Reiki healing.

After retiring from City College in 2003, Diane spent three months in Bali and India practicing yoga, meditation and Classical South Indian dance. In 2006 she settled in Santa Cruz, California, where she continues to teach T'ai Chi Chih, to write, and to photograph the natural wonders.

Made in the USA
Charleston, SC
12 February 2017

The
Healer
Is You